Cunt (kŭnt) n.
A Declaration of Independence

Inga Muscio

Seal Press

Cover design by Ingrid Emerick
Text design by Maren Costa
Author photo by Rebecca McBride

Credits are listed on page 271, which constitutes a continuation of the copyright page.

Library of Congress Cataloging-in-Publication Data
Muscio, Inga.
Cunt: a declaration of independence / Inga Muscio.
Includes bibliographical references.
1. Women. 2. Women—Social conditions. 3. Women—
Psychology. 4. Women—Identity. 5. Body, Human—Social
aspects. 6. Sexism in language. 7. Feminism. I. Title.
HQ1233. M87   1998   305.4—dc21   98-31063
ISBN 1-58005-015-8

Printed in Canada
First printing, November 1998

10   9   8   7   6   5   4   3   2   1

Distributed to the trade by Publishers Group West
In Canada: Publishers Group West Canada, Toronto, Ontario
In the U.K. and Europe: Airlift Book Company, London, England
In Australia: Banyan Tree Book Distributors, Kent Town, South
Australia

In Loving Dedication:

To everyone with a cunt.
Especially, She who persuaded me from Hers:
my Sacred Mother.
I thank you for giving me life.

Contents

Author's Note

Unless otherwise stated, throughout this book the words "gentleman," "man" and the like are used to refer to the tightly knit, male social power structure as it is recognized in American patriarchal society.

Let it be known that the author is fully cognizant of the fact that many men in this world strive for women's rightful place in society. Without the work, study, love and support of certain members of the male sector of humanity, this book would not have been as thoroughly articulated as it was.

The author is grateful and indebted to many members of this sector of humanity, both living and dead, of which her loving father, brothers, nephew, Malcolm X and Robert Graves are merely six.

That said, the author is free to talk some serious shit.

Cunt

(kŭnt) n.

Introduction

"Cunt" is very arguably the most powerful negative word in the American English language. "Cunt" is the ultimate one-syllable covert verbal weapon any streetwise six-year-old or passing motorist can use against a woman. "Cunt" refers almost exclusively to women, and expresses the utmost rancor.

There's a general feeling of accord on this.

Except for some friends who know all about this book, no one calls me a "cunt" to communicate what a cool and sublime human being they think I am. Up until a certain time in my life, I never employed "cunt" to express respect or admiration.

I qualify these statements because my relationship with "cunt" is no longer what it once was.

One day I came home from third grade and asked my pops, "What's a wetback?"

With resignation and a sigh, Dad elucidated a brief history of "wetback." He concluded, "Don't you *ever* say it."

A list of words I was similarly not to utter was forthcoming:

nigger, beaner, kike, wop, jap, injun, spic. The only formal cuss word included on his roster was "cunt."

Coming as I did from a family where us kids were allowed to strew profanities like rice at a wedding, I was mighty affected by all this. Why, in my father's way of thinking, could I call someone an asshole but not a wetback nigger cunt?

The foreshadowings of a mystery.

In my childhood home, the 1965 Random House Dictionary was as much a part of dinnertime as laughter, arguments 'n wanton table manners. Throughout dinner, my siblings and I were required to spell and define new vocabulary words. It was a custom I enjoyed very much.

I was raised to appreciate the power of words.

Little did I know that when I grew up, out of the billion and one words in the 1965 Random House Dictionary and beyond, there would exist no word that I could use to adequately describe myself.

This wouldn't be much of a problem except that there are millions of me's: articulate, strong, talented, raging, brilliant, grooving, sexy, expressive, dancing, singing, laughing women in America, of all shapes, hues, ethnicities, sizes, sexual orientations and dispositions.

We are everywhere.

But what are we.

The only dimly representational, identifying term that advocates truly authentic recognition for the actual realities of women in this world is "feminism." This is a relatively youthful word. Our actual realities, on the other hand, are rooted deep.

We are born with them in our hearts.

Inherited them from our mothers.

Grandmothers.

Under the influence of this dilemma, I've asked myself if there might be a word as old, as universal and as deeply rooted as women's actual realities in patriarchal society. Hidden somewhere in the English language, could there be a word with power steeped in our history, a word which truly conveyed the rage and hope of *all women?*

And lo and behold, I return to the one formal cuss word on Pop's roster:

cunt.

This book is about my reconciliation with
the word
and
the anatomical jewel.

In Part I of *Cunt,* "The Word," I assert that the context in which "cunt" is presently perceived does not serve women, and should therefore be thoroughly re-examined.

English is considered the "universal language" because it represents the victors of history's present telling. Seizing this language and manipulating it to serve your community is a very powerful thing to do, and—based on a variety of specific elements, such as ethnicity, musical tastes, credit limits and/or sexuality—it is done a lot in America. Creating a general, woman-centered version of the English language, however, is just insanely difficult.

Womankind is varied and vast.

But we all have cunts.

While one word maketh not a woman-centered language, "cunt" is certainly a mighty potent and versatile contribution. Not to mention how *deliciously satisfying* it is to *totally snag* a reviled word and elevate it to a status which all women should rightfully experience in this society.

When viewed as a positive force in the language of women—as well as a reference to the power of the anatomical jewel which unites us all—the negative power of "cunt" falls in upon itself, and we are suddenly equipped with a word that describes all women, regardless of race, age, class, religion or the degree of lesbianism we enjoy.

Part II, "The Anatomical Jewel," examines why having a cunt in this society might just be worse than being called one. Our cunts bleed and have weird, unpredictable orgasms. The birthing process is painful and messy. Lordisa knows what our cunts are up to. Generally speaking, we don't understand them, we don't like them and we often think they're ugly.

A different, more sublime way of looking at this is that our cunts are the symbolic and physical zenith of our existence.

When our cunts bleed, *we* are *bleeding people*. Clairvoyant dreams visit our sleepytime heads. Sometimes, the swaggering braggadocio of human males causes our wombs to clench up in spasms of pain. When cunts have stupendous orgasms, we may reel for days, and have a fetching smile for every person we meet when we're walkin' down the street. When cunts get filled up with sperm, women sometimes get pregnant and experience either the trauma of aborting, or the courageous and under-appreciated tribulation of devoting *the rest of our lives* to another human being. When men fuck our cunts against our will, we often feel like a diarrhea shit has been offed upon the very essence of our soul, and may live *the rest of our days* cleaning it off in whatever way we see fit.

An aisle in all American grocery stores is devoted to various commercial products, dreamed up by corporations owned and operated by men, which are designed to "care for" and deodorize cunts. An entire branch of Western medicine, male style, exists because of the infernal, confounding magic of cunts. Doctors who treat cunts have special names.

Famous cunts in history have caused empires to rise and fall.

Sex industries throughout the world enjoy exorbitant profit margins because of the wonderful things cunts do and represent.

When women endure cultural customs such as clitoridecto-mies, chasity belts, Mississippi Appendectomies (i.e., forced sterilization), infibulation, forced prostitution, slavery and rape, cunts are where? Why, in the spotlight, of course.

Yes, though they often play supporting roles to cocks, cunts deserve star billing in the marquee of every woman's life.

Cunts are very important.

Unfortunately, cunts are important to all the wrong people for all the wrong reasons.

Cunts are not important to women because they are the very fount of our power, genius and beauty. Rather, cunts are important to men because they generate profits and episodes of ejaculation, and represent the precise point of vulnerability for keeping women divided and thus, conquered.

History, the media, economic structures and justice systems have led women to the understanding that delighting in a love affair with our cunts will get us no further than Sitting Bull, had he opted to have a passionate love affair with the Seventh Cavalry.

Which, of course, he did not.

Why should Sitting Bull love the Seventh Cavalry? The Seventh Cavalry consistently represented the undoing of his people.

Why should women love our cunts? They, too, consistently represent the undoing of our people.

The main contention here, of course, is that the Seventh Cavalry did not reside between Sitting Bull's legs.

"The Anatomical Jewel" makes up the bulk of *Cunt*. The fact that women learn to dislike an actual, undeniable, unavoid-able physical region of ourselves results in a crappy Sisyphean situation, warranting an intense focus of attention.

Part III is called "Reconciliation." One definition of reconcilia-tion is the re-establishment of a close relationship that has experienced estrangement somewhere along the line.

My cunt is *mine*.

In order to re-establish a close relationship with my cunt, I must take responsibility not only for what it is to me today, but for everything it has become due to the seemingly endless throng of spin doctors, past and present. My cunt serves me in ways *cavernously* unrelated to generating profits, procuring episodes of ejaculation in males and representing the precise point of vulnerability for keeping women divided and thus, conquered. It is therefore my responsibility to insure this reality resides at the forefront of humanity's consciousness when history is rewritten once again.

We women have a lot of responsibilities.

Here are a few:

Seizing a vocabulary for ourselves.

Actively teaching ourselves to perceive cunts—ours and others'—in a manner generating understanding and empathy.

Taking this knowledge out into the community.

Learning self-protection.

Seeking out and supporting cuntlovin' artists, businesses, media and role models.

Using our power as consumers.

Keeping our money in a community of cuntlovin' women.

We arrive at reconciliation by confronting learned, internalized misogyny and re-educating ourselves on our terms. Three of the most important aspects of reconciliation involve fighting with our minds, art and money to create a cultural consciousness that supports and respects all women. The power and potential of these weapons—minds, art and money—are exalted in Part III.

Closing Regards

One of *Cunt*'s aspirations is to contribute to a language and philosophy specifically designed to empower and unite *all women*.

I do not, however, expect my personal experiences necessarily to pluck on the heartstrings of said *all women*.

I am white, so many complexities of individual and
institutional racism are not present in this book like they would
be if I were, say, a Filipina-American writer whose ancestors
founded a ranch outside Houston before the treaty of Guadalupe
Hidalgo was signed in 1848.

I am a lesbian who wouldn't oppose a tumble in the hay
with my housemate's boyfriend's twenty-year-old brother who
lives in Peru and is *achingly* beautiful, so likewise with rigid
strictures of hetero- and homosexuality.

I am an American citizen from a mid-middle-class family
that was supported solely by the sweat of my mother's brow. As
such, I have never been without shoes, food, education, shelter
and other fine trappings of subsistence.

When I was three, an accident with a street-cleaner bristle
blinded me in my right eye. I've lived through the deaths of my
father and youngest brother. I started writing as a child to
survive a spiritually blighted landscape. I obsessively devoted
my life to writing so I wouldn't go insane after my brother died.
I'm a vegetarian, but I like watching people eat spareribs.

All this greatly influences my perspective.

As does a prayer my mother has hanging in her kitchen,
now, then and in the hour of her death: "You are a child of the
universe, no less than the trees and the stars. You have a right to
be here, and whether or not it is clear to you, no doubt the
universe is unfolding as it should."

From the poetry of Sappho to the zines of riot grrrls,
personal experience has proven to be a very effective way for

women to communicate. Sharing individual knowledge contributes to the whole, and has been a foundation of women's power, in cultures spanning the globe, since time out of mind.

Here in America, at the dawning of the post-patriarchal age, a growing understanding of our differences and commonalities continues to emerge full force. Because we now have more means to communicate than ever before, histories based on personal experience are increasingly poised to unite *all women*.

Women are blue-black as the ocean's deepest knowledge, creamy-white 'n lacy blue-veined, freshly ground–cinnamon brown. Women are Christian motorcycle dykes, militantly hetero Muslim theological scholars, Jewish-Chinese bisexual macrobiotic ballerinas and Chippewa shawomen who fuck not just lovers, but Time and Silence too.

Women are drug addicts, anti-abortion activists and volunteers for Meals on Wheels. Women have AIDS, big fancy houses, post-traumatic stress disorder and cockroach-infested hovels. Women are rockstars, Whores, mothers, lawyers, taxidermists, welders, supermodels, scientists, belly dancers, cops, filmmakers, athletes and nurses.

There are not many things which unite *all women*.
I have found "cunt," the word and the anatomical jewel, to be a venerable ally in my war against my own oppression. Besides global subjugation, our cunts are the only common denominator I can think of that *all women* irrefutably share.

We are divided from the word.
We are divided from the anatomical jewel.
I seek reconciliation.

Part I

The Word (wûrd) n.

On the choice occasions popes and politicians directly refer to female genitalia, the term "vagina" is discreetly engaged.

If you will be so kind, say "vagina" out loud a few times. Strip away the meaning and listen solely to the phonetic sound. It resonates from the roof of your mouth.

A "vagina" could be an economy car:

"That's right, Wanda! Come within five hundred dollars of the actual sticker price, and you'll win this! A brand new *Chrysler Vagina!*"

Or a rodent:

"Next on *Prairie Safari,* you'll see a wily little silver-tailed vagina outwit a voracious pair of ospreys."

Say "cunt" out loud, again stripping away the meaning. The word resonates from the depths of your gut. It *sounds* like something you definitely don't want to tangle with in a drunken brawl in a dark alley.

A "cunt" could be a serious weather condition:

"Next on *Nightline,* an exclusive report on the devastation in Kansas when last night's thunder cunt, with winds exceeding 122 miles an hour, ripped through the state."

Or a monster truck:

"The City Arena is proud to present the Coors Crush 'Em

Demolition Round-Up competition, where Randy Sam's *Beast of Burden* will challenge Mike Price's undefeated *Raging Cunt* in the 666 barrel jump."

Moving from phonetics to etymology, "vagina" originates from a word meaning sheath for a sword.

Ain't got no vagina.

Cuntist Mystique

I came across the power of "cunt" quite accidentally. After writing an article for a newspaper, I typed in "word count," but left out the "o." My editor laughingly pointed out the mistake. I looked at the two words together and decided "Word Cunt" seemed like a nice title for a woman writer. As a kind of intraoffice byline, I started typing "Word Cunt" instead of "word count" on all my articles.

The handful of people who saw hard copies of my work reacted strongly and asked why I chose to put these two words on my articles. After explaining my reasoning to editorial assistants, production magis, proofreaders and receptionists, I started wondering about the actual, decontextualized power of "cunt."

I looked up "cunt" in Barbara G. Walker's twenty-five-year research opus, *The Women's Encyclopedia of Myths and Secrets,* and found it was indeed a title, back in the day. "Cunt" is related to words from India, China, Ireland, Rome and Egypt. Such words were either titles of respect for women, priestesses and witches, or derivatives of the names of various goddesses:

In ancient writings, the word for "cunt" was synonymous with "woman," though not in the insulting modern sense. An Egyptologist was shocked to find the maxims of Ptah-Hotep "used for 'woman' a term that was more than blunt," though its indelicacy was not in the eye of the ancient beholder, only in that of the modern scholar. (Walker, 1983, 197)

The words "bitch" and "whore" have also shared a similar fate in our language. This seemed rather fishy to me. Three words which convey negative meanings about women, specifically, all happen to have once had totally positive associations about women, specifically.

Of the three, "cunt" garners the most powerful negative reaction.

How come?

This was obviously a loaded question to be asking myself, 'cause the answer evolved into quite the life-consuming project.

According to every woman-centered historical reference I have read—from M. Esther Harding to bell hooks—the containment of woman's sexuality was a huge priority to emerging patrifocal religious and economic systems.

Cunts were anathema to forefather types. Literally and metaphorically, the word and anatomical jewel presided at the very nexus of many earlier religions which impeded phallic power worship. In Western civilization, forefather types practiced savior-centered religions, such as Catholicism. Springing forth from a very real, very fiscal fear of women and our power,

eventually evolving into sexual retardation and womb envy, a
philosophy and social system based on destruction was culled to
thriving life. One of the more well-documented instances of this
destruction-oriented consciousness is something called the
Inquisition. It lasted for over *five hundred years*. That is how
long it took the Inquisition to rend serious damage to the
collective spirit of non-savior-centered religious worshippers.

The Inquisition justified the—usually sadistic—murder,
enslavement or rape of every woman, child and man who
practiced any form of spiritual belief which did not honor
savior-centered phallic power worship.

Since the beginning of time, most cultures honored forces
which were tangible, such as the moon, earth, sun, water, birth,
death and life. A spirituality which was undetectable to any of
the human senses was considered incomprehensible.

One imagines victims of the Inquisition were not hard to
come by. Women who owned anything more than the clothes on
their backs and a few pots to piss in were religiously targeted by
the Inquisition because all of women's resources and possessions
became property of the famously cuntfearing Catholic Church.
Out of this, the practice of sending "missionaries" into societies
bereft of savior-centered spiritualities evolved.

Negative reactions to "cunt" resonate from a learned fear of
ancient yet contemporary, inherent yet lost, reviled yet re-
demptive cuntpower.

Eradicating a tried and true, stentorian-assed word from a
language is like rendering null the Goddess Herself.

It's impossible.

Ancient, woman-centered words and beliefs never, like, *fall off the planet*. Having long done taken on a life of their own, they—like womankind—evolve, and survive.

Chameleon style.

For women this has involved making many, many concessions, such as allowing our selves, goddesses, priestesses and words to be defined and presented by men.

Many words found in woman-centered religions, such as cunt, bitch, whore, dog, ass, puta, skag and hag, along with the names of just about all goddesses—over time—assimilated bad connotations. As matrifocal lifestyles became less and less acceptable, "cunt" survived, *necessarily* carrying a negative meaning on into the next millennium.

Words outlive people, institutions, civilizations. Words spur images, associations, memories, inspirations and synapse pulsations. Words send off physical resonations of thought into the nethersphere. Words hurt, soothe, inspire, demean, demand, incite, pacify, teach, romance, pervert, unite, divide.

Words be powerful.

Grown-ups and children are not readily encouraged to unearth the power of words. Adults are repeatedly assured a picture is worth a thousand of them, while the playground response to almost any verbal taunt is "Sticks and stones may break my bones, but words will never hurt me."

I don't beg so much as command to differ.

For young girls in this society, coming into the power we are born with is no easy task. As children, our power is not culled out of us as it is for boys. Still, culling power is—above and beyond all social conditioning—a very surmountable *task* to which womankind collectively rises higher each day.

But we need a language.

A means of communication demands and precedes change.

I posit that we're free to seize a word that was kidnapped and co-opted in a pain-filled, distant past, with a ransom that cost our grandmothers' freedom, children, traditions, pride and land. I figure we've paid the ransom, but now, everybody long done forgot "cunt" was ours in the first place.

I have lived the past couple years of my life writing a book called *Cunt*. When people ask me what I do, sometimes I bypass the whole conversation and say I'm a taxidermist. Reactions to a book called *Cunt* always lead to an intense grilling. Ain't never encountered ambivalence. At this juncture, I am still absolutely unable to gauge reactions to this word.

Living with the title of this book as such a huge fixture in my day-to-day life has been a very weird anthropological study unto itself. "Cunt" is a bad, bad word, but *damn* if it don't *intrigue* people when it's the title of a book instead of a meanspirited expletive.

Since everybody already knows that the diabolization of "cunt" is an absolute reality of our language, nobody has to waste time and energy defending its honor.

A cunt by any other name is still a cunt.

"Cunt" is a highly satisfying word to utter on a regular basis.

Every girl and lady who is strong and fighting and powerful,

who thrives in this world in a way that serves her, is a rockin',
cuntlovin' babe doing her part to goad the post-patriarchal age
into fruition.

"Cunt" is the crusty, disgusting bottle in the city dump pile
that is bejewelled underneath and has a beautiful genie inside.

Here is a nice story about the transformation of destructive
negative, crap-ola into constructive, positive brilliantiana.

Once upon a time, civil rights activist Dick Gregory went
into a restaurant and ordered some chicken. Three or four men
who wore pointy white hoods for their nighttime fashion
statement presently came into the restaurant and said, (I'm
paraphrasing here) "Yo, boy. Anything y'do tah dat chicken,
we're gone do tah yoo."

Mr. Gregory looked at the chicken on the plate before him
and was silent.

The men repeated, "Anything y'do tah dat chicken, boy,
we're gone do tah yoo."

Everybody in the restaurant stopped what they were doing
and stared.

Mr. Gregory sighed, picked up the chicken and gave it a big
ol', sweet ol' kiss.

Perhaps, as some "historians" may have it, I fabricated the
historic considerations in reassessing the way we presently
perceive "cunt."

Even if "cunt" were simply four spontaneous letters
someone strung together one day 'cause his wife didn't have
dinner on the table when he got home from a hard day's labor

offing witches or indigenous peoples, it is still *our word.*
Demographically, the women who have *no chance* of negatively
being called "cunts" throughout life can be found in totally
cloistered nunneries and maybe Amish communities.

Based on the criteria that "cunt" can be neither co-opted nor
spin-doctored into having a negative meaning, venerable history
or not, it's ours to do with what we want. And thanks to the
versatility and user-friendliness of the English language, "cunt"
can be used as an all new woman-centered, cuntlovin' noun,
adjective or verb.

I, personally, am in love with the idea.

Part II

The Anatomical Jewel

(j o͞o ´ əl) n.

an eentsy bit of math

If it were my job to mathematically figure out which women despise more: being called a cunt or having one, I'd be hating life.

I'm glad that is not my job.

Instead, my job at present is to discuss some of the different ways 'n means women learn to hate our cunts, which still isn't the most savory task on earth, but it is attainable.

Women comprise over 50 percent of this country. Women comprise just over 50 percent of this planet. There's plenty of power in numbers. If we don't have power, it can't have anything to do with mass.

I conclude it must have to do with some stuff inside ourselves.

To know oneself *truly* is to love oneself. Whereas women do not learn the veritable nature of ourselves in this culture, the likelihood that we love ourselves and/or one another is highly suspect.

All cunts belong to *all women*.

The responsibility sits between our legs.

Blood and Cunts

One fine spring day, after the lunchtime recess in sixth grade, Miss Cothran announced that all the boys were to join Mr. Rogers out on the playground for a game of softball, while all us girls were mandatorially invited to accompany her to the cafeteria.

My friends 'n me knew what was up. We had heard about the infamous Period Movie around fourth grade. Most of the boys were no less familiar with this legendary film and teased us relentlessly as they filed out to the softball diamond.

In the cafeteria, the girls from Mrs. Wolff's class, Mr. Rogers's class and mine assembled into tittering rows. The school nurse stood in the front of the room, between the pull-out movie screen and a table displaying all of the various disposable bleeding paraphernalia we would one day come to know so well. She explained the ways to affix pads to our panties and dabbled a little into tampondom; then the Film Projector Monitor was called to do her duty, and the Period Movie started.

To date, it is the most intellectually impaired film I've ever seen, taking into account the *combined* fatuity of *Basic Instinct* and *Ace Ventura: Pet Detective*.

A cartoon of the female form demonstrated how this dot in your head travels down to your cunt and makes you bleed. The doctorly sounding male narrator insisted that we not take baths or exercise during this "special time," but be sure to keep *spotlessly clean* with lots and lots of soap and showers because menstruating girls tend to stink up the room if they're not completely at one with personal hygiene. He also informed us that any pain or discomfort we might feel resided "in our heads," and had been collectively imagined by womankind for thousands of years.

Were we told anything about how our uteruses are almost exactly like the moon, shedding their linings, growing new ones and shedding all over again? Did the Period Movie teach us *thing one* about how miraculously cool and sublime the human body's reproductive system is when you're a girl?

Fuck no.

All I truly gleaned from this experience was that my cunt was the yucksville reason I had to sit in that stupid cafeteria watching some hack nurse show me how to safety pin a three-mile-wide wad of cotton to a pair of brief underpanties even my grandma wouldn't be caught dead in, while the other half of the sixth grade population was out in the sunshine playing softball. This was the first formal instruction in estrangement from my cunt—within a lifetime's barrage—that I consciously recall.

With all the prepubescent hoopla surrounding periods, I was inclined towards totally vivid nightmarish visions of complete humiliation that would usher in my initiation to

the anatomical jewel

womanhood. A recurring one was related to the shower scene Carrie endured—where she was pelted with tampons—in the Hollywood/Stephen King rendition of menstruation commence-ment. I was *wholly unprepared* for the simplicity and intuition I encountered at the inauguration of my blood.

In seventh grade, I was walking home from school with Teresa Greco and Joyce McCullough. We were halfway down Tunnel Street and suddenly I *knew* I was bleeding. It was the first time I remember *knowing* something in this manner. I told Teresa and Joyce, "Hey, I just started my period," and that was that. I went home, grabbed a pad out of my mom's store and bled on it.

Tampons didn't come along until my fourth period, when Amy Ajello instructed me in great detail over my teen talk phone line. It was tricky holding the phone to my ear and inserting a tampon for the first time but, thank god, I managed, 'cause pads creeped me out the door. Whenever I wore one, I imagined Jimmy Vallejo and Andrew Vasquez pointing at the gigantic bulge moshing up my ass as I walked down the hall. In my vision, they howled, à la Beavis and Butthead, and everyone else, of course, would hear about it and I'd be the laughingstock of the whole middle school.

Shame kept a close watch on me and all my girlfriends.

It was shameful to bleed, to be seen bleeding, for blood-soaking paraphernalia to be visible on or about one's person at any time whatsoever, to speak of bleeding, to look like we were bleeding, to be excused from P.E. because of the crippling cramps which sometimes accompany bleeding, to display frailty, vulnerability or mood swings because we were going to be bleeding soon and to express any emotion other than contempt and disdain in reference to our blood.

No one, least of all my peers—who, verily, whispered about this proscriptive subject in hushy undertones, behind closed doors, in only the most trusted of boyless locales—thought bleeding a pleasant reality.

Girls are told bleeding is a *bad thing,* an *embarrassing thing,* a *secret thing* that we should hide and remain discreet about come hell or high water.

Boys are told to go outside and play sports while the girls learn about some creepy, cootie-laden mystery that makes blood ooze out from our you-know-whats.

Given my swimmingly fetching cultural milieu, getting used to this bleeding business took quite a while. In the meantime, I fervently asked people why the hell this happened to us girls. Various sources consistently informed me that it was (big sigh) "just part of being a woman" (big sigh), or the good ol' standby curse we inherited from Eve.

My period was not only a "curse," but for the first years of bleeding, I was completely incapacitated with mind-numbing spasms of pain. For at least one day out of every month, I didn't go to school or work. I lay in bed and cried, unable to do anything about the agony of my uterus. Frequently, because of this "imagined" pain, I fainted and puked.

I find it fascinating that men's description of the pain enkindled by a knee to the groin sounds awfully similar to what I have experienced for up to thirty-six unflagging hours. And yet, imagine the hue and cry if men were informed that the

the anatomical jewel

horrifying symptom of pain accompanying a swift kick in the
nuts was purely psychosomatic.

A coupla years after my period started, the newspapers
across our fair nation announced that women *weren't* imagining
those intense pains. *Scientific studies* proved that the pain *is real!*
As you might surmise, this was but a *load* off my mind.

After all those days I vomited because the mid-section of
my body was clenched in a fist of throbbing excruciation; when
I sat in the bathtub crying for five hours straight; when I
couldn't get out of bed or leave the house for fear of fainting in
public; suddenly, because a group of men took the time to study
a group of women and found there was indeed a rational reason
for these symptoms to wrack our bodies once a month, I was
allotted the pale comfort of knowing this pain *actually* existed!

Oh, joy.

Cynic that I am in such arenas of contemplation, I wonder
if perhaps this generous allotment wasn't bestowed upon
womankind because pharmaceutical companies came to the
magnanimous conclusion that sales for pain relievers would
skyrocket if only they invested in a little "research" to counter
the "in her mind" myth and re-condition the general public into
believing there was a veritable malady at hand.

In the spring of 1995, I had the momentous honor of inter-
viewing Barbara G. Walker at her home in New Jersey. Among
many other things, she told me about menarche parties
women in her community have for the newly menstruating.
Ms. Walker described a menarche she attended a few months
prior to our interview. The honoree wore a red dress. Her

mother made a beautiful, red cake for her. A bunch of women, young and old, brought her red gifts wrapped in red paper. The older women talked about the symbolism of the moon and the miraculous joys of both bleeding and not bleeding anymore, while the younger women who hadn't yet started to bleed duly expressed reverence for the honoree, and enthusiasm about starting their periods.

I mean, wouldn't that be wonderful?

Wouldn't you feel like a total princess if your mom or whoever did that for you? Wouldn't that put a whole new slant on bleeding from the get go?

I was deeply moved by Ms. Walker's account, but in all honesty I must acknowledge my bittersweet envy. My mom's a dang smart lady, and I admire her above and beyond all women on the planet, but it was a bummer to realize that if she hadn't been so busy dealing with the social constraints of single motherhood during the early '80s, sans the aid of a supportive community of women, she might have had the inspiration to hostess a menarche for my sister and me. Whereupon, I sincerely doubt I would've spent almost a decade of my life teaching myself to love the blood that coursed out my stunning cunt every month.

Throwing menarche parties for our younger sisters, nieces and daughters is a very simple and profound way of effecting positive change for the next generation.

Get off your ass and do it.

If Pippi Longstocking were the nation's covergirl, rest assured that women would have a superlative role model in the fine

science of accepting ourselves. Ms. Longstocking is extremely
outspoken in response to negative social beliefs:

> [T]he children came to a perfume shop. In the show window
> was a large jar of freckle salve, and beside the jar was a sign
> which read: DO YOU SUFFER FROM FRECKLES?
>
> "What does the sign say?" asked Pippi. She couldn't
> read very well because she didn't want to go to school as
> other children did.
>
> "It says, 'Do you suffer from freckles?'" said Annika.
>
> "Does it indeed?" said Pippi thoughtfully. "Well, a civil
> question deserves a civil answer. Let's go in."
>
> She opened the door and entered the shop, closely
> followed by Tommy and Annika. An elderly lady stood back
> of the counter. Pippi went right up to her.
>
> "No!" she said decidedly.
>
> "What is it you want?" asked the lady.
>
> "No," said Pippi once more.
>
> "I don't understand what you mean," said the lady.
>
> "No, I don't suffer from freckles," said Pippi.
>
> Then the lady understood but she took one look at
> Pippi and burst out, "But, my dear child, your whole face is
> covered with freckles!"
>
> "I know it," said Pippi, "but I don't suffer from them. I
> love them. Good morning." (Lindgren, 1970, 18-19)

Unfortunately, Pippi Longstocking is *not* the nation's
covergirl.

✻

All the way through my teens and into my twenties, I loathed my period. "Menstruation" was synonymous with unmitigated physical pain on a monthly basis.

But then I got to thinkin'.

Maybe because I was in college, and what are you supposed to do in college if not think? Maybe because I noticed a marked difference in the way women reacted toward menstruation at this point in human development. Maybe because for the first time in my life, I found myself surrounded by women who were greatly intrigued by the workings of our bodies. Maybe because by the time I went to college I'd taken enough psychotropic plant forms to feel more or less At One with the Universe, instead of lost at sea in the swimmingly fetching cultural milieu I'd previously more or less accepted as reality.

During this period of thinking, I read books and watched the moon.

All women throughout time have had the *opportunity* to see the moon. From Africa and Asia to the Americas and Europe, plenty of these ladies started noticing that the moon grows, recedes and grows again, over and over every twenty-eight days. Those not detached from their menstrual cycle couldn't help but trip out on how their own blood rhythm also occurred over the span of approximately twenty-eight days.

This is how the moon links one up with a form of history none of the textbooks can possibly touch upon: a *psychic* history with all the women who've ever bled on this planet.

By reading some books, investing in a lunar calendar and poking my head out the window every night or so, I figured out how to tell time by the moon. I learned her phases and moods. The springtime full moon has a much different luminescence than the autumntime full moon. When I went to a party on a dark moon, I generally had a shitty time. When I went to a party during the moon's waxing phase, or better, when it was full, I had a whopping good time.

And on and on.

Soon after me and the moon got to be buddies, the strangest thing happened. The simple act of *hanging* with the moon invoked beliefs my brain had never computed before. Suddenly, all the period propaganda shoved down my throat since that fateful day in sixth grade was far away and beyond ridiculous.

Lo and behold, my period stopped hurting!

I designated the first day of my blood a Special Time where I consciously guarded my quiet. I soaked in mineral salted baths, read Pippi Longstocking, mended clothes (before this, shortening a skirt involved the use of duct tape and an iron) and cooked Creole Tomato Soup.

I quit taking ibuprofen. My period mellowed out even more. For the first time in my life, I actually *enjoyed* bleeding. I gauged myself with the movements and rhythms of the moon. I still got cramps, but I didn't faint or puke at all.

Hip, hip!

One month I had pretty bad pains and took some ibuprofen. The following month, the pain was even worse. Then I did an experiment. Some months I took pain relievers and some months, I didn't. Every time, the month *after* I took pain relievers, I'd have, as Holiday Golightly would say, the Mean Reds.

Though the medication brought *immediate* relief, the following period was excruciating. Taking menstrual-pain drugs became a vicious cycle. I never realized it before, and it was so obvious once I saw it, but I needed more and more ibuprofen to keep the pain at bay each month.

This little experiment resulted in an *absolute mistrust* for everything I had ever learned about being a woman in this culture. I began the arduous task of questioning, re-evaluating, researching and rewriting the entire information-cataloging system in my brain.

For two years, I did not watch television, read newspapers or any magazines which did not reflect a standard of womanhood with which I identified. Dr. Leo Daugherty, one of my esteemed instructors at the Evergreen State College, told me that for one whole year he read books only by women writers, and I did that too.

All this activity started with my period, but it soon encompassed my entire life and history as well as my way of perceiving the lives and histories of every woman with whom I came into contact.

The way I had learned to deal with my bleeding ways was a reflection of what our society teaches us about everything cuntlovin' and female and rhythmic and sexual. These are things which must be somehow "controlled" with shame, embarrassment, taboo, violence or drugs. In order to serve the destructive tendencies of our society, everything that is cuntlovin' must be sequestered away far into deep recesses of the collective unconscious *somehow.*

Therefore, like our cunts, our blood is weird, messy and ugly. The negativity surrounding menstruation is an illusion that falls, falls, falls away the instant perspective shifts.

And all this mental activity started with me and the moon.

The moon has consistently proven herself to be every woman's ally since the beginning of time. The moon renders fearful illusions of social conditioning petty riffraff that gets in the way of a cuntlovin' lady's life. The moon fucken rules.

Once you decide your body is your fine-tuned hot rod to tool you around this earth as you desire, buy a lunar calendar (I highly recommend the one published by Luna Press). Put it where you'll see it every morning. Slap it up by the coffee maker, the bathroom mirror or above your bed. Wherever. Look at it every day. Notice where the moon is on the calendar. As often as possible, notice the moon in the sky. That's all you have to do, nothing fancy, just notice the moon. The clincher here is *consistency*. Watch the moon grow and recede every month. Be able to eventually wake up in the morning and know where the moon will be that evening without looking.

This is aligning yourself with the moon. Since, like I say, the moon has been teaching us ladies about our insides since we developed the eyeballs able to see that high, there's no wrong way to do this. The moon will teach you just as it taught your distant ancestors.

When you get your period, make a (red) mark on your moon calendar. What did the moon look like when you got your period? What did it look like last month? Sooner or later, you'll get a rhythm going with the moon. You'll have your period every

new moon or every waxing moon, or maybe one month you
will get your period on the full moon, the next month on the
waning moon, next on the new moon and next on the waxing
moon. It varies just fantastically. There is no way of knowing
what your cycle is until you lunarly track it. Even then, it is
likely to traverse the moon's phases throughout the year, but if
you keep a good record and watch what goes on between your
cunt and the moon, you'll be able to predict, *to the day*, when
you start your period, *even if you are "irregular."* Again, I can't
stress enough: This takes time. You may not have a full grasp on
your cycle for six months or even longer.

Patience is this: a virtue.

As you begin to groove with your fine cunt workings and
the moon, you'll be able to perform all kinds of neat-o miracles.
You can figure out if you're in for a hellish period. Nasties like
yeast infections can be easily nipped in the bud because you're
so *utterly hip* with yourself. What were once faintly clairvoyant
premenstrual dreams take on more lucid clarity and depth. Sex
becomes more intense and ecstatic. Menstrual cramps diminish.
You can determine when you will and won't get in the family
way—if you investigate the matter fully.

Our society creates a hospitable climate for cuntpower to be
generated into profits amassed by large corporations. Pharmaceutical and feminine hygiene companies, plastic surgeons and
weight-loss centers are designated to care for our bodies in our
stead. We learn to rely on various "experts" and authority figures
who patronizingly inform us how we should respond to our
bodies. We are not offered the opportunity to consider how we'd

like to respond to bleeding, nor are we presented with how women menstruated in the past or in other cultures.

Becoming responsible is about quitting the "expert" addiction, feeling and listening to what is going on inside of us and responding in ways that feel good and right to us. Learning to be responsible for your body *takes time*. It's taken you *all your life* to learn how to alienate yourself to the point of total irresponsibility.

If it took society, say, twenty-five years to teach you that you have no control, it'll take you less than a tenth of that time to learn yourself otherwise. In the long run, that's not much time at all, but still, it does indeed amount to roughly two point five years.

It is of utmost importance to be patient with yourself, your ignorance and your curiosity. Any stockbroker in her right mind will tell you: The return on an investment is wholly dependent upon the investment itself. By the time we're twelve or so, society has convinced the vast majority of women that it is in our best interest to remain incontestably oblivious to our bodies, outside the realm of tormenting ourselves into reflecting a certain standard of physical beauty. Therefore, it is entirely reasonable that we never pause to invest in ourselves on terms that we ourselves define. Our subjugation continues because women are estranged from our actual realities.

Taking responsibility for one's bleeding ways is part of the reality-based revolution founded between the soft, luscious thighs of every woman on the planet.

A more material aspect of this revolution is downsizing the percentage of our funding to corporations that exist for no other purpose than to constrain women in the throes of body-alienation and perpetuate our deleterious relationships with our cunts.

Here is my story about that.

I went to Anystore U.S.A. to buy a box of tampons. I had but eleven dollars to my name. I went down the aisle where I would find "feminine hygiene" products, bitterly playing that term through my mind.

Why are words like "hygiene" and "sanitary'—which imply that a woman's cunt is unclean—acceptable in our society? Why are these people trying to sell me feminine deodorant spray? That's like hawking floral air freshener to a lady who lives in a rose garden.

Also, excuse me, but what's so clean about dicks?

One never hears of sanitary jock straps, deodorant condoms, perfumed Hershey-Squirt protection pads or hygienic ball wipes, whereas I've heard tell of need for such products.

So anyway, with thoughts such as these playing through my mind, you can imagine my dismay on tampon-buying excursions. If I happen to be in a good mood, it's simply annoying. If I happen to be in a bad mood, I am a green monster who lives in a trash can with a grand piano. On this occasion, I was in a bad mood.

I grumbled down the aisle, openly sneering at all the products on the shelves. New Freedom this and Light Days that.

Comfort, security.

Plastic applicators.

Discreet disposal pouches printed with flowers that do not exist.

I positively *fumed* as I scanned the prices. Five, six, seven bucks for *a box of cotton*. Sixty, seventy bucks a year.

Why the *flying fuck* should a woman have to *pay* some huge corporation over and over because the lining of her uterus naturally, *biologically* sheds every month?

Amongst my small circle of friends, I tally seven hundred dollars spent on tampons and pads a year. I estimate the women in my apartment building spend thirteen thousand dollars a year to swell the already enormous profit margins of "feminine hygiene" companies.

Reluctantly, I made my selection: a box of Tampax Slender Regulars for $7.19. I stormed my way to the check-out line. In front of me was a young man who said hello.

I replied, "Do you realize that I will have barely three dollars in the whole wide world after I purchase this box of tampons because my period is coming and I find it unsavory to bleed in all my clothes and on every seat I occupy for the next few days?"

He told me that he'd considered this very conundrum. His girlfriend had bitched about the same thing at length.

We fell into a check-out line conversation on the matter, comparing men's hygienic expenses to those of women and also, how the moon is totally disregarded in our culture in relation to womb-type activities.

The couple behind us—a well-to-do looking pair in their lawn-bowling sixties—kept clearing their throats, saying ehh-hemmm and harrummphh. The woman, especially, gave me extremely disdainful looks for speaking so tactlessly and loudly in the Anystore U.S.A. check-out line.

A few days later, I related this experience to my friend Panacea Theriac, who, at the time, had just organized a small women's health collective in Olympia, Washington.

She said, "Oh, Inga! I've been using sea sponges! Have you heard about them?"

I said no.

Panacea told me all about them. She bought three sea sponges for $1.59 apiece. Besides their obvious economic virtues, she said, you use them over and over, so they're more ecologically desirable; when your sponge gets soaked with blood, no matter where you are, you just haul it on out, wash it real good with hot water and mild soap, then pop it on back in; you never have to trouble yourself with remembering to bring a tampon reserve; they're totally comfortable and fun to play with in the bathtub. Also, you can squeeze the blood out into a jar, fill it with water and feed it to your houseplants, who, Panacea assured me, "absolutely adore the stuff."

I asked her about Toxic Shock Syndrome and whether sea sponges harbor yucky things that can make a girl sick.

Panacea said that it is very, very important to keep your sponge *super duper clean*, washing it thoroughly every time you use and re-use it.

Trusting my friend as I do, I bought a couple of sea sponges at the local health food co-op and gave them a whirl. The only problem I've had is that when a sea sponge is full, it is *full*. If you laugh or yell when the sponge has absorbed its maximum capacity, your nice white panties will get a big red how-do-you-do on them.

Other than that, sea sponges are the coolest. I've developed an endearing friendship with my sponges. They are miraculous little plant bodies that once lived in the ocean, which is also ruled by the moon. And they don't carry that impersonal, flushable, bleached personality tampons possess.

Sea sponges can be found at almost all Anystore U.S.A.-type stores, usually in the make-up or bathtime section. If you're lucky enough to have a health food co-op in your town, they're sure to have them. At under two dollars apiece, they pay for themselves after one month.

Keep them clean. Boil a new sponge before you use it for the first time. Store them in a little cotton bag. Wash them and let them dry completely before putting them away for the month, but *always* wash them again before using. I've heard that you can use more than one at a time if you bleed a lot, but I've never tried this. I wouldn't recommend using the same sea sponge for more than a few months because the natural fibers wear down after a while and it gets kinda disintegratey.

A friend of mine who uses sea sponges once told me about an experience in a public restroom. She was at a busy nightclub, waiting in line with eight or so other women to use the toilet. There were four stalls and at least that many women at the sinks, primping and washing their hands. Suddenly, all normal bathroom conversation came to a crashing halt as a voice from behind one of the stall doors pealed out, "I'm coming out with my sea sponge, so if you're gonna gross out, shut your eyes." A woman then emerged from her stall, sea sponge in hand. With all eyes upon her, she washed it carefully at the sink, went back into the stall and finished up her business. One woman actually did close her eyes, but everyone else stood transfixed, witnessing the woman's ritual with her sea sponge. When the woman came out again, she fielded quite a number of questions about where to get sea sponges and how to use them. The whole room of women came together for a few moments, laughing and talking about our blood.

I enjoy imagining how the culture of restrooms would be different if our periods weren't all hush, flush 'n rush.

Using sea sponges is one very good way for women to cut down on contributions to large corporations that don't readily promote the idea that cunts are sacredholy, and responsible for the entrance of every human being walking this earth.

But some ladies just don't like internal blood-soaking devices at all. Some ladies like to bleed *onto* something.

Even though me and my period have come to terms quite nicely over the years, I still can't put anything up my cunt on the first day of my period. My uterus rebels if a stray pubic hair finds its way up my canal on that ultrasensitive first day.

So I asked my grandmother, "What did ladies bleed on before Kotex dreamed up those thick-as-white-wall-tire pads and elastic security belts?" She blinked her desert tortoise eyeballs before replying, "Child, where do you think the phrase 'on the rag' comes from?"

So smitten was I with not spending my money on tampons, I started safety-pinning rags to a pair of boys' underwear. (Why are BVDs so comfy, while Maidenform makes all these panties that cost too much and skooch up one's ass?)

I cut up a towel for my rags: A few are around four inches long and six inches wide, and the rest are five inches long and two inches wide. I wrap the wider width rags around my underwear, placing as many of the thinner ones between the

the anatomical jewel

45

wide rag and the underwear panel as I'll be needing.

It takes some practice to figure out how to get the rags situated just so. I can't really offer any suggestions, as it depends on how much you bleed, how you walk, sit and stand, what kind of fabric you choose, how you decide to affix the rags to the undies, etcetra and etcetra.

Many health food stores sell ready-made flannel rags with velcro fasteners.

If you sew, design your own rags.

If you don't sew, contact Blood Sisters. Their address is in the Cuntlovin' Guide at the back of this book. Heck, this organization is *so dang cool*, get in contact with them, regard-less. Blood Sisters features a line of cuntlovin' bleeding products, a zine, gorgeous t-shirts and an entirely cuntlovin' blood-o-centric philosophy.

And then, of course, there's the trusty Blood Towel.

I've had the same Blood Towel for seven years. It is blue. Terra cotta shadows stain it everywhere.

Linus from *Peanuts?*

Me and my Blood Towel.

When I'm on my period I sleep with my Blood Towel between my legs. We all know you're not supposed to wear tampons or sea sponges to bed, and rags and pads always seem to mosh up the ol' ass. Maybe a Blood Towel isn't the most alluring thing to wear to bed, but it sure is comfortable and keeps the sheets clean.

In the morning I walk around the house with my Blood Towel wrapped around my waist. It catches the flow when I sit down. I use it to wipe the insides of my legs. Otherwise, the blood splatters on my feet, the floor. I step in it and get it everywhere.

Sometimes I don't clean it up right away.

Messy, messy. Fingerpaints in kindergarten messy.

I like to do this for a very good reason:

Because I can!

Isn't it amazing.

By the simple act of not wearing panties, I can stand in the middle of my kitchen and *change the way it looks*. Without moving a muscle, a pool of blood appears between my feet.

Like magic.

Bleeding on sea sponges, rags and Blood Towels may *seem* undesirable when affiliated with commonly accepted standards for absorbing blood flow. But these "inconveniences" are founded solely upon our indoctrination in this society. Spending time with your blood is a constructive action. Bleeding every month is a part of life that we are taught to ignore. When we choose, literally, to *see* it, we open up to our actual reality as cuntlovin' women.

Rinsing a sea sponge out in the bathroom of a fancy restaurant or washing bloody rags by hand may not be as "convenient" as flushing all one's cunt ambrosia away into the city sewer system, but it reconnects a cuntlovin' woman with her body and, indirectly, with the bodies of every cuntlovin' woman, living and dead, who has ever known the sensation of blood flowing out of her cunt.

You have a ritual for bleeding on throwaway cotton. *You and only you* know your bleeding technique. Sure, it takes time

47

to learn another one but the nice thing is:

Human beings are the most highly adaptable mammals on the planet. You'll figure out a system.

If, for example, you were to decide that using rags and sponges was impossible except when you are home at night, that'd still cut your dependency on large corporations' products anywhere from 20 to 50 percent.

In some situations, I use tampons (preferably, the un-bleached kind found in food co-ops and healthy rainbow sister stores). But instead of being *solely reliant* on tampons, instead of coughing up the money every single period, it takes me three to five months to empty a box.

When I *unconsciously* relegated the right to be in charge of how I bleed to various commercial and corporate entities who have no interest in me as a living being, much less as a woman, the distribution of my power did not serve me. Feminine hygiene corporations fund the lives of a small percentage of men who *remain* in power because they are so good at convincing us ladies that the most *natural and convenient* thing for us to do is to give them ours.

Speaking of men.

As individual husbands, fathers, brothers, sons and lovers, rather than as the most affluent team of business associates on the planet—are involved with this bleeding situation in a deeply subconscious way.

Men do *themselves* a *great service* learning about women and the moon. Unless they're incarcerated, it is just about impossible to avoid interacting with us.

Bleeding ladies are taught to be, at best, intolerant of a month-to-month physiological occurrence which clocks the time of our bodies. We therefore act mighty peculiar. Disliking something unavoidable takes its toll after a while. Some people call this PMS.

If, at every stage of life, society commanded men to despise their hard-ons, how pleasant would they be when this bodily function that they are incapable of desisting occurred?

Society fails to acknowledge that our bleeding cycle affects men's lives tremendously. This is further compounded by the fact that women who live or work in close proximity to one another tend to merge bleeding cycles. Chances are, every woman in a given household or workplace is bleeding at the same time. Sometimes men are surrounded on all sides by cranky, bleeding cunts.

To the incognizant, we seem entirely unpredictable. We may bite a man's head right off for the smallest vagrancy.

They know this.

There is no way for them not to know this.

But chances are, they don't understand, and act like jerks 'cause their courage is tested. When most men who don't understand women see how really scary we are, courage usually segues to fear. This results in anger, frustration, violence and the perpetuation of general disrespect towards women. Bottom line: Men are afraid of our blood.

How's this for some serious chicken shittedness:

Keep away from women in their courses,
and do not

the anatomical jewel

49

approach them until
they are clean.
But when they have
purified themselves,
You may approach them
in any manner, time, or place,
Ordained for you, by God.
(*The Koran,* Sura II, 222)

The ancient world's most dreaded poison was "moon-dew"
collected by Thessalian witches, said to be a girl's first
menstrual blood shed during an eclipse of the moon. Pliny
said a menstruous woman's touch could blast the fruits of the
field, sour wine, cloud mirrors, rust iron, and blunt the edges
of knives. If a menstruous woman so much as laid a finger on
a beehive, the bees would fly away and never return. If a
man lay with a menstruous woman during an eclipse, he
would soon fall sick and die. (Walker, 1983, 643)

Can't say that I blame men for fearing our bloody cunts. We
be powerful people when we bleed.

When women bleed, all of the frustration and anger we've
stored in our bodies for the month is physically manifested in a
sudden and swift change in hormone levels, resulting in an
openness and vulnerability that cannot be described. Menstruation is a monthly purging and cleansing. We hear, taste and
smell things that are usually indiscernible. Whether we consciously recognize it or not, we feel threatened when our
heightened senses are assaulted.

I assert that menstruating women intuitively want to be *left alone* or with other bleeding women, as many of our great-great grandmothers firmly believed.

A number of societies certainly have the right idea prohibiting highly sensitive menstruating women from entering churches where a son-sacrificing, war-mongering, sadistic god is worshipped. Unfortunately, this prohibition is enforced because of the belief that menstruating women are "unclean" and not because we'd rather spend the sabbath quietly paying homage to ourselves and the moon.

A few friends and I spoil each other silly if we're hanging out on the first day of someone's period. We fry up sweet 'n sour tofu, give massages, play Toni Childs and Sade or bring each other chocolate-covered strawberries. Mostly, we sit quietly and stare out the window and demand absolutely nothing of each other.

The social requirement that we fulfill the responsibilities of our non-menstruating selves at all times throughout our cycle is the source of our alleged PMS.

We're taught to distrust everything about our very compelling blood mystery. Yet the clickety-clack, passive-aggressive business world of men and machines is the absolute antithesis of everything our senses crave on the first few days of our blood. In our souls, we still know this. In our DNA, we want to be quiet with ourselves. In this society, where a day to ourselves might very well mean no one to care for the children and no food on the table, bleeding women are naturally irritable.

The evils of our blood recede when—however fleetingly— we're free from the demands of this unfeeling world. When we

the anatomical jewel

sit reverent and peaceful. When those around us respect our silence. This is when the negative becomes positive.

Every woman has a different way of honoring her blood.

Every so often, Bambi, my housemate, has a ritual of painting fantastic gold leaf menstrual homages, framed in total baroque. Bambi's not a painter, she's a musician. Her period tells her when it's time for another painting. "I seem to make one every eighteen months or so," says Bambi. She has no idea why she started painting with her menstrual blood in gold.

Some women cook fabulous dinners for themselves, some save up money to take in a weekend by the sea.

When you open yourself up to learn how to honor yourself, the *how* part just falls into place via your imagination, passion and lifestyle.

It takes a lot of time, focus and energy to realize the enormity of being the ocean with your very own tide every month. However, by honoring the demands of bleeding, our blood gives something in return. The crazed bitch from irritation hell recedes. In her place arises a side of ourselves with whom we may not—at first—be comfortable. She is a vulnerable, highly perceptive genius who can ponder a given issue and take her world by storm. When we're quiet and bleeding, we stumble upon the solutions to dilemmas that've been bugging us all month. Inspiration hits and moments of epiphany rumba 'cross de tundra of our senses. In this mode of existence one does not feel antipathy towards a bodily ritual that so profoundly and routinely reinforces our cuntpower.

Reproductive Control for Cunts

Just because I don't envision myself in a romantic, sexual
relationship with a man anymore, doesn't mean I
never have.

The first time I got pregnant, I was
nineteen and living in the agricultural
community on the California coast where I'd
lived all my life. A mere two weeks separated
me from my move away from home to Seattle.
Making such a major move with a tiny human growing inside my
body seemed a pretty contradictory way of setting off on my own.

The thoroughly unsavory "option" of hanging around town
for nine months and then giving my child to an adoption agency
didn't hold my attention for more than two puffs off the continuous cigarette I'd had in my mouth since I got back my test results.

So I went to Planned Parenthood for a clinical abortion.
In the waiting room, there always seemed to be fifteen or
twenty other women, no matter how many left with the nurse.

Evidently, it was "abortion day."

We were shuffled through the clinic like beef cows. All of
the women had the same horror-stricken, empty look on their

faces. It was one of those situations where one can assume one holds the same expression as everyone else without looking in the mirror. I sat there for an hour and a half, nervously leafing through *People* magazine, in a desperate attempt to give a rat's ass about the lives of Darryl Hannah and Whitney Houston.

When they called my name, I probably would have shit my pants if there had been any digestion going on in my intestines, which there wasn't. It's hard to eat when you're pregnant with a child you do not want.

My boyfriend accompanied me into the exam room. I was told to strip and lay on the table, feet in the stirrups. I still remember the ugly swirl designs and water marks on the ceiling. After a while, the nurse came in and explained what would be happening.

She referred to the machine used for clinical abortions as a "suction device," which is a more professional way of saying "vacuum cleaner." In theory, if not design, this machine is quite like the Hoover Upright, the Dust Buster or the Shop-Vac in your closet at home.

The nurse didn't mention how useful vacuum cleaners are for cleaning up messes. In our society, a pile of kitty litter on the floor is treated much the same as an undesired embryo. The main difference, though hardly recognizable to Western science, is that kitty litter is sucked from cold linoleum and an embryo is sucked from a warm-blooded living being's womb.

Instead, because I was crying like *La Llorana,* she said, "Are you sure this is what you want?"

What other goddamn choice did I have?

I muttered, "Just do it, please."

With the ugliest needle I'd ever seen, she shot something

into my cervix. I don't think my cervix was residing under the belief that it would someday have a large needle plunged into it, and so protested accordingly. The pain was overwhelming; my head swam into the netherworld between intense clarity and murky subconscious.

Then I heard a quiet motor whirring.

The lady told me to recite my ABCs.

"A, B, C, D, E . . . " Something entered my cunt, deeper, deeper, deeper than I imagined anything could possibly go.

"F, G, H, I, O, W . . . " The walls of my uterus were being sucked, felt like they were gonna cave in. I screamed, "O, P, X, X, D, VOWELS, WHAT ARE THE VOWELS? R? K? A! A's A VOWEL!" And then my organs were surely being mowed down by a tiny battalion of Lawn-Boys.

"S, did I say S?" My boyfriend was crying too, didn't tell me whether I said S or not.

There was a white-wall-tire pad between my legs then, and blood gushed out of me. The motor had stopped whirring. I was delirious. I asked, "What do you do with all the fetuses? Where do they go? Do you bury them?" The lady ignored me, which was fine, I had to puke. She led me into a bathroom and I vomited biley green foam. Then I went to a recovery room, lay down and cried.

There was another nurse woman in there, she patted my hand, reassured me, "I know just how you feel."

"You've had an abortion before too?"

"No, but I know how you feel."

I told her to get the fuck away from me.

For two weeks, there was a gaping wound in the center of my body. I could hardly walk for five days.

Then, stupid me, a couple of years later, I got pregnant again. I still lived in Seattle, but was just about to move to Olympia, to begin school at Evergreen.

I couldn't really envision myself having an academic edge with a bun in the oven, so I faced the reality of going to that machine once again. This time I was more terrified than before. I knew all too well what that rectangular box and its quiet motor had planned for my reproductive system.

Have you any idea how it feels to willingly and voluntarily submit to excruciating torture because you dumbly forgot to insert your diaphragm which gives you ugly yeast infections and hurts you to fuck unless you lie flat on your back anyway? I was to withstand this torture because I was a *bad girl*. I didn't do good. I fucked up.

I had the same choice as before, that glowing, outstanding choice for which we ladies fight tooth and nail: the choice to get my insides ruthlessly sucked by some inhuman shitpile, not invented by my foremothers, but by someone who would never, ever in a million years have that tube jammed up his dickhole and turned on full blast, slurping everything in its path.

Abortion #2 took place in a clinic that was under so much political pressure, I wasn't even allowed to recuperate. Twenty minutes after the vacuum cleaner was out of my body, I was dressed and walking home.

Felt like a piece of shit.

On one of Olympia's main thoroughfares is an abortion clinic. I passed it every day on my way to and from school. Almost always, there were old women, young girls and duck hunters standing on the corner outside the clinic, holding signs in their hands showing you pictures of a dead fetuses with some words underneath to the effect that this may have been the next president of the United States of America.

Whenever I saw those people out there, especially the young girls, I'd see myself yanking the bus cord—in all probability, snapping it in two—vaulting off the bus, crossing the street and morphing into a walking killing machine, kicking in faces, stomping on hands. There were times when I gripped my wrist so I wouldn't yank that cord.

At this point in my life, I'd begun to study different kinds of medicines and healing methods. One thing I learned in college was that knowledge helps me transcend anger. Upon examining my desire to physically assault individuals whose convictions were in direct opposition to mine, I delved into histories and applications of medicines far and wide. At the same time, I was hanging around with a group of women who were asking a lot of compelling questions about our reproductive systems. We found many of the readily available answers to be thoroughly unsatisfactory, and started discovering our own.

In this research, we found one constant: healing starts from within. It appeared to be some kind of law. No, more than a law. Is breathing a law? Is waking up every morning a law? If so, maybe the notion of healing coming from within is a law as well.

I had never been comfortable with the idea that healing comes from the physician or his bag of tricks, because I learned years before, when I had my own health challenge with polio that healing has only one source. The doctor can

the anatomical jewel

57

aid the body by removing foreign particles, injecting chemi-
cals, setting and realigning bones, but that does not mean
the body will heal. In fact, I am certain, there has never
been a doctor anywhere, at any time, in any country, at any
period in history who ever healed anything. Each person's
healer is within. The doctor is at best one who has recognized an individual talent, developed it and is privileged
enough to be able to serve the community by doing what he
does best and loves doing. (Morgan, 1991, 91)

This concept is completely alien, even deviant, in our culture.
In this society, we look to the outside for just about everything: love, entertainment, well-being, self-worth and health. We
stare into the TV set instead of speaking of our own dreams,
wait for a vacation instead of appreciating each day, watch the
clock rather than listen to our hearts. Every livelong day we are
bombarded with realities from the outside world, seemingly
nonstop. Phones, car alarms, pills, coffee, beepers, ads, radios,
elevator music, fax machines, gunshots, bright lights, fast cars,
airplanes overhead, computer screens, sirens, alcohol, newspapers. One hardly has the opportunity to look inside for love
and peace and other nice things like that.

Western medicine, that smelly, deaf dog who farts across
the house and that we just don't have the heart to put out of its
misery, is based on a law opposed to the one the rest of the
universe seems to go by, namely: Healing Has Nothing to Do
with You, Just Follow the Directions on the Label.

In America, we don't (nor are we encouraged to) look
inside ourselves for healing, finding truths or answers. If you

want to know something, you find out what the Person in Charge of This Area says. The weather is not to be discerned by looking at the sky, the mountains in the distance, or by listening to the song of the wind. You will find it in the Report of the Meteorologist. And likewise, if you are pregnant and don't want to be, you don't look to yourself and the immediate, personal resources in your immediate, personal world, you pay a visit to the Abortionist, who will subsequently predict the climate in your body for two weeks, guaranteed.

And so, la dee dah, once, twice, three times a cuntlovin' lady, I got pregnant again. It was the same boyfriend as the other two times only now we were breaking up. It was the fuckedest one of all because I didn't want to be with this man and I shouldn't have fucked him, but it was his birthday and he was obviously fun to romp with and blah dee blah blah blah. No force on earth could make me feel like I wanted this child. Furthermore, I promptly decided there was to be no grotesque waltz with that abhorrent machine.

So, I started talking to my friends about abortion alternatives. I lived in a small town with a high population of like-minded cuntlovin' women, so that was one thing in my favor right there. Against me was the fact that I was eight weeks along, which is too advanced for an organically induced miscarriage. According to naturopathic physician Loraine Harkin, six weeks of pregnancy is the outside limit for herbal abortions. Since they are effective about 60 percent of the time, she says it's important to schedule a surgical abortion since a fetus is most sensitive to the harmful effects of herbs and drugs in the first eight weeks of pregnancy. I made an appointment at the women's clinic (the one with the protest-ers, who'd since moved on to haunt other neighborhoods) as a back-up in case my way didn't work out.

My dear friend Judy, the masseuse and scientist, was my biggest resource. She and Panacea found some herbal tea recipes a Boston anarchist-feminist group printed. (I tried to contact this group, but they had evidently disbanded.)

Judy came to my house almost every night and massaged my uterus where you are not supposed to massage pregnant women who want to keep their babies. She also did reflexology by rubbing either side of my Achilles tendon on both feet.

I knew a naturopath in Olympia, who was one of my sources of inspiration in learning about healing from within. She taught me this thing called "imaging." It may sound terribly New Age, but through imaging, I got rid of this weird bump I'd had on my labia *all my life*. Since imaging goes on in your own head, I can't tell you how to do it specifically. The basic idea is: *Every* night, when you are falling asleep, graphically imagine the part of your body that's giving you problems *changing*. For the bump on my labia, I imagined all this beautiful soft flesh growing over and absorbing the bump. When I was pregnant, I *vividly, consistently* (I do believe these are the operative words when imaging) imagined the walls of my uterus gently shedding.

Eight days passed from when I started inducing miscarriage to the morning my embryo plopped onto the bathroom floor.

Judy's daily massages and my continuous imaging of the lining of my uterus shedding away at every moment of my days, I feel, were *the most crucial* elements of my success story. I was absolutely focused on miscarrying and I *felt* Judy's gentle, yet firm massages prodding things along quite nicely.

It was an incantation.

Me and my women friends did magic.

Esther's love made magic. She supported me and stayed with me every day. Bridget's thoughtfulness made magic. She brought me flowers. Possibly most magical was the fact that, after the first coupla days, I possessed not one filament of self-doubt. With that core of supportive women surrounding me and with my mind made up, I was pretty much invincible.

I stress this because in America, we tend to hold that popping medicine in our mouths and swallowing is the extent of our involvement in the healing process. We believe that if we get better, it's because the *medicine* worked magic, not the *person*. Many women I know have tried to induce miscarriage and failed because they took certain herbal potions and went about their lives as if everything were normal, waiting for the herbs to work their wonders. To successfully induce miscarriage, one must devote One's Entire Life to the attainment of this goal. *I place an enormous amount of emphasis on this point.* When I induced miscarriage, I breathed, ate, shat and slept thinking of nothing else but the lining of my uterus shedding.

The herbal teas and other oral and topical applications I prescribed to myself were *little helpers*. They served to further direct *my own focus* and *aid* me in achieving my goal. Herbs are *particularly* good little helpers because plants easily and synergistically jive with one's own magic and are quite willing to work with you if you respect them.

The herbs I chose were blue cohosh root and pennyroyal

leaves. The information I am providing is to illustrate how I, *one specific individual*, induced a miscarriage. There are hundreds of emmenagogues and abortifacients that grow on the planet. The two I decided to use were chosen after a lot of dicussion and reading.

After a week of non-stop imaging, massages, tea drinking, talking and concentrating, I was brushing my teeth at the sink and felt a very peculiar mmmmbloommmp-like feeling. I looked at the bathroom floor and there, between my feet, was some blood and a little round thing. It was clear but felt like one of them unshiny superballs. It was the neatest thing I ever did see.

An orb of life and energy, in my hand.

And Jesus H., wasn't I the happiest clam? It hardly hurt at all, just some mild contractions. I bled very little, felt fine in two days. I wore black for a week and had a little funeral in my head.

Organically inducing a miscarriage was definitely one of the top ten learning experiences in my life thus far.

You know, it's like when Germany invaded Poland. I once read how in the ghettos of Warsaw, the people fighting the Nazis were real amazed at first that a Nazi soldier would die if you shot him. They *suspected* that Nazis could die, but *felt* like they were somehow superhuman.

That's how I felt after I miscarried a child without paying a visit to the beef cow clinic and that sickening vacuum cleaner. I felt the way I imagine any oppressed individual feels when they see that they have power and nobody—not men and not their machines—can take that away.

Terminating a pregnancy in any manner is a harrowing, traumatic experience. At the time, my emotions were an odd juxtaposition of untold grief and profound exhilaration. When the sadness settled quietly into my heart, I felt *so happy* to be a woman. I looked at all my women friends with such an intense, burning rush of joy. My cuntlovin' friends and I did something *amazing* to *affect my destiny* in the most conducive possible way.

I learned that the fight for human rights does not take place on some bureaucratic battleground with a bevy of lawyers running from congressional suite to congressional suite, sapping resources into laws. The war for peace and love and other nice things like that is not waged in protests on the street. These forms of fighting are a reaction to oppression, giving destructive power that much more energy. The real fight for human rights is inside each and every individual on this earth.

While traversing along this particular train of thought, I realize I just might sound like a woman who has never experienced the unspeakable horror of back-alley abortions, and I am. I also realize that it might seem as if I'm ungrateful to all the cuntlovin' women who fought their hearts raw for legal abortions, which I am not. The fact that there now exists a generation of women who can actually consider clinical abortion to be an oppressive diversion from our own power is *based wholly upon* the foundation that our mothers and sisters built for us. I sincerely thank the individuals who fought so hard that I may have the luxury of the belief I now hold. Evolutionarily speaking, it is quite natural for this fight to progress into a new arena, for the fight is not over, it has not ended. The squabble between pro-lifers and pro-choicers serves only to keep our eyes off the target, and nothing more.

Without the women in my life, both living and dead, I

would have been roadkill simply ages ago. All women benefit
from concentrating our energy on the power within our own
circle of friends, creating informal health collectives where we
discuss things like our bodies and our selves.

Abortion clinics, in their present incarnation, will be
completely unnecessary when we believe in our own power,
and the power of our immediate communities. The abortion
issue can become a personal, intimate thing amongst cuntlovin'
women friends.

Can you say Amen.

Nobody here is saying abortion is a form of birth control.

It isn't.

Having an abortion totally sucks. Practicing a birth control
lifestyle is a fabulous all expenses paid, carte blanche vacation
in Tahiti compared to terminating a pregnancy.

Birth control is preventative medicine (referring, of course,
to the nurturing, woman-centered definitions of "medicine"). It
is actively sustaining a lifestyle that grosses and nets the fewest
possibilities of conceiving a child. Having an abortion, on the
other hand, is terminating the progress of something that is
already quite under way.

However, since the morning-after pill has been cleared by
the American Food and Drug Association, abortion and birth
control have kinda merged a bit.

The morning-after pill was not available to me the three
times I was pregnant. If it had been, I do not know if I would
have taken it, because I am deathly fearful of pills, and am
unclear on the long-term side effects we're talkin' here. There

is definitely an allure in a pill one can take "just to be safe."
Absolute knowledge of conception is a non-issue. Take the pill,
have your period, and if it's a little heavy and clotty, figure ya
mighta been, but then again maybe not.

Kinda preventative, kinda terminator style.

Yeah, the morning-after pill runs 'long a misty boundary.

One thing I'm pretty certain about, though. Featuring this
pill as a fabulous star in one's birth control lifestyle would rend
untold—quite possibly irreparable—damage to the lining of one's
uterus. Since it's now accessible, I am concerned that women
could start relying on it too heavily.

My opinion of the morning-after pill also runs along a misty
boundary. It's damn important for a lot of reasons. But to the day I
keel over, I'll be a diehard, furrow-browed skeptic whenever male-
run industries are involved with us womenfolk's business.

That said, I know of three birth control lifestyles that are 100
percent safe and infallible.

The first—abstinence—is no fun and extremely unhealthy,
so forget that one.

Masturbation *is* fun. Lordisa, is masturbation fun. It's also
liberating, empowering and a superlative form of safe sex. You
cannot get pregnant or become HIV positive even if you are in a
circle jerk with everyone and her sister. Besides all of these
outstanding qualities, masturbation is an *absolutely peerless* cure
for the hiccups.

Masturbation is a high art. I have a cuntlovin' friend who
masturbates without touching herself. She ornately concentrates
on an erotic adventure until she comes her brains out. She's

rolled her eyes and moaned on public transportation and in long lines at the grocery store. Comin' her brains out. Another friend of mine goes the manual route, but has specialized her timing and precision in elevators.

For those of us less mentally talented and/or dexterous, there are vibrators, dildos, Ben Wa balls, butt plugs and massage wands shaped like everything from dill pickles to elephants with trunks raised clit high. Also, of course, the five holy and munificent fingers on each hand.

Sex exclusively with girls is also fun. Unless pregnancy is on the agenda, or something immaculate occurs, lesbians do not usually conceive. Women do not have sperm. Thus, women cannot accidentally get each other pregnant. HIV, though, is another scenario. Women are able to pass HIV to each other. The research done thus far on the possibility of acquiring HIV woman to woman is inconclusive, but the risk should be taken seriously. Trust no one but yourself, and always practice the safest possible sex.

In conclusion, the only 100 percent safe and infallible birth control lifestyles worth considering are: masturbation and/or sex exclusively with women. When neither of these lifestyles coincides with a cuntlovin' woman's reality, the prevention of unplanned pregnancy is often an issue.

There are ways for cuntlovin' women to deal with this issue without the pill, barriers against the cervix, hormone implants or whatever other "choices" male-centered medicine's birth control industry has palmed off on us.

What, exactly, is the lifecycle of a *woman's* body *doing* under the jurisdiction of a medical science established, defined and implemented by people who *do not have cunts?*

It's like suddenly, one day in the Middle Ages, people figured men should be in charge of women's bodies since they were in charge of pretty much everything else.

In context, at the time, perhaps it made sense.

It does not make sense anymore.

Maybe we lost contact with our archives somewhere along the way. Maybe we kinda went ahead and played along like we were dumb. Maybe we got beaten and raped and tortured and enslaved into submission.

That is the past.

It's something to reckon with, but also: it's gone.

Face it, forget it.

Focus on the present: the age of communication.

We gots us the Internet.

You can e-mail government officials in Pakistan and plead mercy for the fifteen-year-old girl sentenced to death for killing the man who raped her. You can find the chemical compound for Depo-Provera and see how that chemical compound affects the human body. You can hop on Diamanda Galás's website and find out what in good Lordisa's name she's up to now. You can download all the recipes for chocolate chip cookies on the planet earth and follow a different one each month when you and your friends are PMSing.

And that's just the Internet.

Living as we do in an age of communication, it is pretty much acceptable to go, "Hey Gramma, what'd you use for birth control, how did you bleed, what was sex like back then, how many lovers did you have, how many abortions, when, where,

the anatomical jewel

how, why?"

Bam, connection with history.

Our communication environment fosters vast, far-reaching and intricate networks of women who utilize fanzines, small presses, schools, record companies, magazines, television shows and movies. Women from all socioeconomic stratas communicate in mediums that in the past were either not accessible or not invented.

It is *perfectly socially acceptable* for you to write down every thought you've ever had about *anything*—from your gorgeous prize wisteria, to the insane relationship you have with your hair, to your all-consuming love for the clitoris—then slap the words together with some cool pictures, make five hundred copies, staple each and sell them to every woman you do and don't know for a buck a pop.

Bam, everybody profits.

All these situations are now in context and they now make sense.

We are able to share knowledge, history, experiences, recipes and remedies like our motherkin could not. As more and more women communicate, a new language and sense of community evolves. Equipped with language, a means of communication and the desire to talk to one another, our voices, histories and dreams whirling dervish into regenerative cuntpower.

The story of you gives the life of me personal power in my body, my eating and health habits, and in my political, spiritual, emotional and ethnic beliefs.

Without you, I am ignorant, oppressed, alone.

Without you, I am powerless.

As we all know, up to this point American women have tended to rely upon methods of birth control founded upon a body of knowledge created by men.

    This holds true, even after it's religiously proven to us like water torture on our foreheads from the cradle to the grave: Men have a vested *financial* interest in controlling our lives, histories and bodies. Men dearly love, cherish and respect women until death do us part as long as we're:

consumer

wife

teacher

helper

bitch

concubine

accountant

housekeeper

orphan

punching bag

counselor

nag

nurse

threeholestopenetrate

cook

mother

daughter

prey

Whore.

Tangle, tangle, tangle, mother, grandmother, sister.

We been told for centuries, he's father, lover, husband, brother, son, and really, truly does have our best interests in mind.

Pa-shaw.

"Our best interests" are naturally, unquestionably pre-defined by a social power structure that, at the turn of the twentieth century, witnessed an ad for *Lysol* with a recipe for douching to keep wives from experiencing "embarrassing odors" during intimate moments with their husbands.

Nowadays, most women who think about this kind of stuff—and have the opportunity—matronize the offices of women healthcare providers. Women go to male gynecologists—I can only imagine—because it's a family tradition or there's no better option. For me, personally, anyone who didn't have a cunt and tried to look at my cunt in an exam room, would get a silly slap upside the head with a cold speculum.

I know women *do* choose to go to male doctors because I see their names in the yellow pages: Richard, Ted, Micahel, James, Peter. I can only assume this means there is a demand for male gynecologists.

I don't know any women who go to male doctors, though.

A lot of women have decided that the whole way we interpret healing in our culture is based entirely on a male construct. These women go to women naturopaths who rely on healing straight from Big Mom's Bosom.

Her thuja oil, for instance, which—with the expertise of a healthcare provider—can cure chlamydia. Her red raspberry leaf tea that tones and strengthens the uterus. Her acidophilus bacteria in yogurt that cures yeast infections by restoring the natural acidity of your cunt.

And then there is you.

You who are a child of the universe. Whether or not it is clear to you, you came from Big Mom's Bosom too. Birth control and health care are very much integral aspects of your spirituality, self-esteem and power. Not only do you have vast wonders of communication at your beck and call, but Big Mom provided you with a mind and a will—the most omnipotent panaceas on the planet—to wield.

The naturopath I mentioned earlier asks new patients to document everything they eat for a week and fully detail personal and family medical histories. On the first visit, she conducts an interview to get the psychological and emotional context before doing *any* physical examination. She procures a whole picture of what's going on before ever touching someone's body. You know: holistic medicine.

This lady taught me a lot.

We learn to respect everything our doctor tells us. Doctor knows best. Perhaps. But the doctor learned about healing in a destructive school of thought. The doctor learned to isolate and napalm physical ailments. Vicariously, through the doctor, we too learn to deal with our bodies and health destructively.

We kill headaches with aspirin, which also weakens immunity to headaches.

Meditation and yoga soothe the stress that causes headaches, while a plethora of herbal teas calm the spirit.

We kill infection with antibiotics, which also weaken immunity to infection.

Keeping cuts clean and drinking lots of fresh water to flush out the system make topical infection a non-issue. Internal infection and viruses are nipped with garlic, witch hazel, cayenne pepper, echinacea, goldenseal, chaparral. These and many other plant substances feed the immune system, which fights its own battles.

Accessing Big Mom's resources, while passionately communicating and accepting your power to heal yourself is constructive-assed, cuntlovin' medicine.

There are two basic, commonly accepted models of birth control. Both are, to greater or lesser degrees, based on the destructive model of "healthcare":

1. Chemical manipulation of the hormones.
2. Barriers placed between the os (opening of the cervix) and sperm.

I will suggest a third method of birth control, based on a philosophy intrinsic to a cuntlovin' woman's life.

Chemicals, i.e., Napalming

Three unplanned pregnancies be damned, I'm gonna go for broke here and assert I'd be hard pressed to come up with more systematic and refined forms of chemically induced oppression than synthetic hormonal birth control products. Birth control pills, Depo-Provera and Norplant all function in pretty much the same way—they control a woman's reproductive cycle by manipulating hormones.

Depo-Provera and Norplant were introduced on the market in the 1990s. It has come to light in recent years that the side effects of hormonal implants are far-reaching and extremely detrimental. Unfortunately, at least a decade will pass before the pernicious effects of these "new developments" are firmly established.

Because the pill is the oldest of the three, more is known about its insidious effects on a woman's body. The pill diminishes sexual desire, causes undue weight gain through laboratory generated manipulation of the hormones, obstructs the natural cycle and menstrual flow, represses ovulation, causes heart problems, irritability and migraines, has been linked, unlinked, re-linked to cancer, and synthetically dictates one's entire physical agenda. The pill creates a constant state of false pregnancy. Women on the pill do not have a natural menstrual cycle. Bleeding occurs when placebo pills instigate a false period.

The reproductive cycles of women on the pill are choreographed and maintained by Ortho-Novum factories.

Depo-Provera and Norplant are simply newer products of an industry that profits from control over women's lives. Any "developments" in the birth control industry will always reflect a cavalier attitude towards our bodies.

A lovely woman named Marcy Bloom, the director of Aradia Women's Health Center in Seattle, Washington, once smoothly countered my rant against the pill. Ms. Bloom's is a very thoughtful and judicious perspective on the issue:

> What you say about the pill is true. However, it is the most successful method of birth control as well—that's the Catch-22.

For some women, the pill is the only method that works, or the only one they're willing to use because either they don't want to touch their bodies, or their lover is very resistant to using condoms. Sometimes the pill is the only psychosocial method a woman is willing to use, because all other methods require a woman to touch herself.

First off, let's get the Condom Matter behind us.

A gentleman who doesn't have the physical and/or emotional sensitivity to use condoms *couldn't possibly* possess the self-confidence required to fully procure the infinite soundings of pleasure from the depth of a woman's being, via the endlessness of her cunt.

At least not with his dick.

Insecurity about a physical lack of sensitivity in their bodies overrides their lover's mental and physical health. Cro-Magnon sociopsychological beliefs (i.e., "Women are the ones who get pregnant—they should deal with birth control.") also contribute to this ignorance.

This says nothing about what kind of dumbass would completely disregard the threat and reality of HIV.

Men who refuse to use condoms do not deserve to be fucked by anyone but other men who refuse to use condoms.

Taking *any* hormonal birth control product because we don't want to touch our bodies beats all our much-needed revolutionary, resurrectionary cuntlovin' synapses into hibernation 'n submission. This makes it difficult for a woman to just plain and simple love being a woman. By encouraging a physical aversion to our own bodies, the pill only adds to the unspeakably large number of ladies inclined towards cunthatred presently existing within the body of womankind.

Loving, knowing and respecting our bodies is a powerful and invincible act of rebellion in this society. This fundamental, entirely crucial act is not possible while we buy into destructive philosophies at the root of hormonal birth control products.

I've had countless discussions with birth control advocates who regard synthetic hormones as a right which allows us freedom.

What is the frame of reference we draw upon to reach this conclusion? Are we not basing this on the experiences of our ancestors who were dicked around, relatively speaking, no more and no less than we are to this day, but had access to quite a bit less information?

The only reason hormonal birth control products are considered a "right" is because women haven't yet decided to construct an entirely woman-based frame of reference with all of the information our ancestors could not communicate to each other through the Internet, zines, books, periodicals, shows, conventions, sporting events, festivals and fax machines.

The main freedom involved in using hormonal birth control is freedom from thinking about—and ultimately facing—our repro-ductive power. This "freedom" essentially results in an ignorance of our bodies which costs us, individually and collectively, dear, dear, dearly. We cannot love ourselves if we do not know ourselves.

There is bliss, but no freedom, in ignorance.

We have the means to educate ourselves and rely wholly upon rights and freedoms that totally jive with the rhythm of womankind in every way. If you are on hormonal birth control products, you *cannot* educate yourself about your body because *your body is not under your own Goddess-given jurisdiction.*

I return to the same argument I offered about using sea sponges, rags and Blood Towels. We've learned to place patriarchal rhetoric at the nexus of our thoughts. We're all reared in a society where the real, honest to goddess power of women intimidates just about everybody. Especially people who, historically and futuristically, have not a hope in hell of seeing blood course out from 'tween their legs, or of giving birth to members of the human race.

What it boils down to is this: If it didn't *originate* with women or the Goddess, if it does not *spiritually, emotionally, physically, psychologically and financially benefit* women, it does not serve women.

So fucken chuck it.

Barriers (Isolation)

Women-initiated barrier methods—such as the diaphragm, cervical cap and various spermicide-soaked sponges—do not eclipse a woman's cycle. A woman using barrier methods ovulates and bleeds. Barrier methods require physical contact with one's cunt, and that's *always* a good thing.

I, personally, have not had good experiences with barrier methods when I've been sexually active with men, which is neither here nor there.

Barrier methods have been used for thousands of years. Lemon halves and sponges or mosses soaked in spermicidal herbs were used by some of our greatest grandmas. Mass-produced cervical caps were around in the 1930s, and home-jobbies were used in many ancient cultures.

The sole reason I am negatively disposed towards the use

of barrier methods is that the industry that creates them is not run by women.

If it were run by women, the following story just could not, ever, happen.

Once upon a time, there was something called the IUD. This stands for intrauterine device. The IUD was implanted in women's uteruses and inhibited the natural growth and shedding of the uterine lining. It made the uterus an inhospitable place for an egg. IUDs caused uterine cancer, infertility and—when they didn't cause death—tore the insides of many women's bodies asunder.

After wreaking havoc on hundreds of thousands of American women's uteruses and lives, an IUD called the Dalkon Shield was finally taken off the market in 1976. This was not an act of graciousness on the part of A. H. Robins (the corporation responsible for the Dalkon Shield). They were removed from the American market because six hundred lawsuits were pending against the company. These six hundred were but a spit in the ocean compared to the 306,931 lawsuits filed by 1986. And these three hundred thousand–plus lawsuits represented a mere 8 percent of women potentially harmed by the device. (Bloss, Cornell, Moon, Tomsich, "The Dalkon Shield," 1997)

Meanwhile, what do you do with 697,000 surplus IUDs? The instruments of terror were sold to USAID (United States Agency for International Development). These 697,000 IUDs were then "distributed"—willingly or not, I couldn't venture to say—to women in impoverished nations, who, unlike American women, did not have the relative luxury of a legal system. (Raymond, 1993, 15)

the anatomical jewel

77

✳

Condoms are a barrier method of birth control I advocate for three reasons: They were designed by and for men, they work, and they are proven to reduce the risk of acquiring HIV.

I've never heard of condoms that make men's dicks shrivel off their bodies. I assert that this is a calibrated reflection of who produces what for whom.

If a collective of women designed a method of barrier birth control, produced it in a women-run company and ran advertisements depicting positive images of cuntlovin' women from all ethnicities and walks of life in women-owned mediums, I would jauntily support it.

At present, however, there is no such method of birth control, and I do not trust the birth control industry. I do not believe the needs of women are taken into consideration at all. I do not like knowing a multibillion-dollar corporation that inherently cannot regard our bodies as holy-rhythmic, gets all its money from us.

The birth control industry is a Big Business. We are mere consumers in this context. Our bank accounts are much, much, much more important than our bodies. If birth control is indeed "the womenfolk's responsibility," let's seize our responsibility with vigor, shall we.

Cuntlovin' Ovulation Alert

In no way do I claim to be a health practitioner.

Nor—as my Macintosh PowerBook with internal modem would gladly testify in a court of law—am I of the Luddite persuasion.

I am a woman and a writer who has thought about and experimented with the workings of her cunt with passion and vigor.

When you start teaching yourself about your cunt, you get a rhythm going. It is your rhythm and only you understand it 100 percent. When you breathe deeply and stay with this rhythm in your body, you will notice it encompasses every aspect of your life.

What I am about to discuss is not "the rhythm method." The objective here is not to understand the rhythm of your ovulatory cycle. The objective is to tap into the rhythm of your ovulatory cycle as a means of perceiving a broader rhythm inside yourself that shows you how powerful you are every day of your life.

Long before physicians started "curing" people with charming procedures like putting leeches all over their bodies, birth control was a normal part of life. There are as many forms of birth control as there are cultures in the world. It wasn't until popes and missionaries preached the sinfulness of sex outside of reproductive purposes for a couple hundred years that people started distrusting their medicinal regimes. Lots of people still practice their own kind of reproductive medicine, only now it's invalidated and called "voodoo," "black magic" or "folk medicine."

The big problem with forms of birth control founded in the people, the plants and the moon is that no one trusts them. They all completely depend on the individual woman and her community in order to be effective.

Few in our society have trusted the individual woman and her community to take absolute control. En masse, women haven't trusted ourselves or subsequently been trusted for over two thousand years.

The nice thing, though, is everything's changing. It's not *impossible* for small groups of women all over the nation to learn about our cunts and trust each other together. In the mite of a moment, we can get online. We can post what we know and find what we're looking for. We can sit in a cafe with our three best friends and discuss our erotic fantasies. We can purchase books that tell us all about our cervix.

Assuredly, the best place to start learning and trusting is the place from which you entered into this world.

Your Cervix: Axis and Ally

Everything your uterus produces—blood, eggs, babies and a variety of miraculous secretions—eventually passes through your cervix before leaving your body.

Your cervix is the doorway of humanity. Have you ever seen it? If you haven't, you dang well should. Viewing your cervix will not be a disappointing experience, I promise on a stack of holy *Beloved*s by Toni Morrison.

Go to your local women's health clinic with probably a five or ten dollar bill. Ask for a small, medium or large plastic speculum, and hand the nice health clinic lady the five or ten dollars. Along with the speculum, ask her to give you an instruction sheet. If you live in one of the more woman-negative states like Utah, Florida, Texas or Mississippi, you may need to purchase a plastic speculum through the mail.

Read the instructions that come with your speculum. If
you're lucky enough to have a supportive women's clinic in your
community, ask any questions you may have before leaving. If
you buy a speculum through the mail, either call the company
you ordered it from, or call the woman-positive health clinic
nearest you by referring to the appendix in *A New View of a
Woman's Body*, a book I vehemently urge you to purchase in a
later chapter.

With your speculum, you can further investigate and learn
of your wondrous cunt. Besides the speculum, you will need a
flashlight, possibly some lube, a hand-held mirror and maybe
some gentle patience. Practice opening and closing the spec a
few times before inserting. Keep in mind that speculums were
not designed for self-exams. It can be frustrating trying to get
that thing to work right the first one or nine times, but try to
relax. Tight cunt muscles don't facilitate this maneuver.

To insert a speculum: Lie down with some pillows under the
small of your back. Spread them legs. Hold your cunt lips apart
with two fingers of one hand. Insert the speculum sideways,
longest handle facing your body. If things are parched down
there, employ the lube, but use it sparingly. One of the main
objectives here is to be able to see your juices in their natural
element. Ya' won't be able to distinguish the lube from the juice
if you lay it on too thick. Once you get the speculum in about
halfway, turn it so it lies flat. Don't open it up when it's
sideways. Gently insert it on in to the hilt and open it up.
Wheee! There's a little lock mechanism on these things; click it
into place when you get it opened as wide as you can.

Mind, this is not *the most comfortable* sensation in the

world, but it shouldn't hurt at all (unless you have an infection
or open sores or something), so long as you don't pinch any o'
that tender skin as you open the speculum. However, if you're
not used to having things in your cunt, especially hard, plastic
things, you may experience more discomfort at first. Keep
trying. Remember to relax.

Once the speculum is in, opened and locked, grab that
flashlight and mirror. If you can't see your cervix, either you
have a long cunt canal or a shy cervix. For the former scenario,
try the exam again just before, right after or on the lightest day
of your period. This is when your cervix is most visible. For the
latter, bear down like you do when taking a shit. That cervix will
overcome its stage fright in a matter of seconds. If lots of flesh is
bulging around the speculum, you probably need a larger size.

Take a good long gander. Note the shape, color and texture
of your cervix. It changes appearance according to where you
are in your cycle. If your cervix looks kinda bluish or is indeed
bright blue, it's time for a pregnancy test. If you're ovulating,
you may see mucous, your cervix will be pulled higher up, it
may be softer and larger than usual and the os may be open
slightly. The os looks like a Q-tip wouldn't pass through it, but it
is altogether capable of dilating to accommodate the head and
shoulders of a new human being.

Cuntjuices: Know Your Ambrosia
Look, touch, smell and taste your cuntjuices. *Never* gross out on
tasting yourself. You are an acquired taste. Acquire it. You
swallow your spit without a qualm millions of times each week.
It's filthy in comparison to your delectable cuntjuices.

This is another very good way of getting a rhythm going. You taste differently when you're about to bleed than when you're ovulating, and it's completely up to you to make distinctions.

A woman's body releases an egg once a month. This egg sits around in your uterus, waiting for some sperm to show up. It is not stupid. After twelve to twenty-four hours, it figures no sperm's gonna take it on a hot date and it makes an exit without further ado.

Sperm can live in your body anywhere from seventy-two hours to five days. What this means is, if some sperm finds its way into your uterus up to *one working week* before your body releases its egg, you *can, feasibly*, get pregnant.

When an egg is present, you are ovulating. Generally, not always, but *generally,* a woman ovulates halfway through her menstrual cycle. Therefore, if you had your period when the moon was new, then there's a good chance you'll ovulate when the moon is full.

Another indication that you're ovulating is a slight twinge of pain in your lower abdomen. It doesn't feel like a menstrual cramp, it's more of a tight, pinched-nerve-type pain. If you masturbate, you can sometimes feel it after you come.

Also, I should probably add that when you are ovulating, you will often become insanely horny. You may feel the urge to couple with the kitchen-table leg, though I wouldn't necessarily take this as an ovulatory symptom.

The *most* reliable way to tell when you are ovulating is by intimately familiarizing yourself with the posh setting of your cunt by interpreting messages from your cervix.

Stick your finger—middle finger's best—up your cunt, swipe it around and around your cervix, being careful not to neglect the underside, where secretions like to settle. If you are ovulating you will find a nice blob of snot on your finger. There's no seemly way to describe this. It's snot, quite unmistakably, plain and simple, snot. It has no odor or color, it's just clear snot, and as such, tastes a little salty. This snot's function is to create a warm, cushiony thoroughfare for sperm to travel to your egg.

The unique characteristics of ovulation snots are created by a rise in the hormone estrogen. Before you ovulate, the discharge on your finger is milky and creamy. Right after you ovulate, when you stick your finger up your cunt, you'll find sticky, tacky, maybe curdy, white stuff. If the sticky white stuff is there, with either a little snot mixed in or no snot at all, figure you just ovulated. Estrogen decreases at the approach of your period and progesterone rises, making your cunt dry up a tad. As you get used to checking your cuntstuff, you'll be able to recognize what's what.

Now, if you're gonna be making expeditions in your cunt with your fingers, *keep those fingernails clipped and wash your hands!* If anybody else is of the mind to explore your cuntal regions with their digits, make goddamn sure they keep their nails clipped and hands clean too. Many minor infections are attributed to the hairline lesions caused by fingernail scratches. If you're prone to these minor infections, examine your lover's fingernails and hand-washing habits.

I've made it my business to peruse my cuntjuices once or twice every week when I'm not bleeding. The best time to do this is while taking a shower, when my hands are already quite clean and I'm already quite naked. I've incorporated this investigation into my shower ritual, so on any given week, I know exactly where I am in my cycle. When you make knowing your cunt's cycle an important part of your *normal* bathroom regime, it becomes rote.

After a few months of familiarizing yourself with your snots and milky or curdy or tacky white stuffs, ask yourself this question: "How can I get with child if I know exactly when I am fertile and, therefore, take precautionary measures?" Precautionary methods may involve the use of condoms, engaging in sexual activities that do not involve dick 'n cunt intercourse or investigating erotic fantasies based on titillation and masturbation.

Cuntlovin' Ovulation Alert is of obvious benefit to women who *want* to get pregnant. It's also a divine service for women who aren't at all preoccupied with the possibility of conception. Your cunt's rhythm affects perspective, mood and creative and erotic expression. What is day-to-day life, but perspective, mood and creative and erotic expression? Knowing and grooving with your cunt is *such* a huge assistance in these matters.

Cuntlovin' Ovulation Alert furthermore helps you:

1. Plan and navigate your way through any given week.
2. Anticipate and deflect negative interactions with people you care about.
3. Love yourself, which in turn effects positive changes for future generations of women. Counting you, that's one more cuntlovin' woman in the world who is contributing to an environment of cuntlove.

c
u
n
t

Cuntlovin' Ovulation Alert dictates compassion and respect for all women.

Once you get to the point where you anticipate what juices your cervix is letting loose, emotional and psychological rhythms inside you become more lucid.

After that, there's no stopping you.

You rule.

We are at the juncture of examining the repercussions of truly, candidly understanding our cunts.

Let's say now you've made some serious decisions about your body. Let's say you've developed a keen interest in reigning at the helm of your body's rhythm. Optimally, let's say you're open to falling in love with yourself in a way you only remotely considered in the past.

According to my little theory, a highly developed sense of compassion for your physical self has a rippling effect in the subconscious. It leads to the development of a psychic sense of compassion for everyone with a cunt. Once you understand your personal rhythm, you intuitively connect yourself with all the people who share a similar rhythm.

These people are womankind.

Which leads us to honoring the single most excoriated group of women in the world.

Not virgins.

Not mothers.

One more guess.

Whores

I am thankful to have been blessed with a fairly well-developed sense of entitlement during the composition of every chapter in *Cunt*.

Except this one.

This one's been difficult.

I've never *been* a Whore.

I've read and thought about and talked to Whores. As a woman living in this society, I'm *consistently reminded* I am a *potential* Whore whenever a man is not escorting me, which is rather most of the time. None of this, however, is the same as consciously *experiencing* Whoredom firsthand. If I were a *truly* resourceful and courageous individual, I would've learned how to be a Whore for subsistence while I wrote this book. Alas, I am an impractical chickenshit in this regard.

Whores are a very important part of *Cunt*. Every time I've tried to explain why, though, I've met this insecurity inside myself. It is a very cranky insecurity that says stuff like, "You don't know what it's like to *be* a Whore, you dang fool. Can't base no chapter on sneaky suspicions."

But Whoredom is a massive part of our history and power as women. When fully instructed in the art of sacred sexual power, Whores are the people who can teach us all the stuff we grow up not learning about sexuality, our bodies and our innate sexual power. Our cultural ignorance and intolerance of Whores keeps Whores from realizing the full potential of Whoredom. It likewise robs women and men of Teachers who can help us understand women's sexual power.

Whores were a central part of religion, spirituality and everyday life in times when the Goddess—a *truly* sexual being—was overtly worshipped. It took a lot of work, study, devotion and commitment to become one of the Goddess's sexual priestesses. People were free to visit the temples of Whores, and did so to learn, to love, to open up physically, to heal.

I ruminated over this chapter for a long time, and prayed the Goddess would help me. Like always, She came through. This time She manifested Herself in a woman named Carol Queen, a writer, sex activist and Whore.

You won't find Carol Queen in the acknowledgment section because I know people don't always read the praises in books, and I want everyone to know:

Carol Queen fucking *rules*.

Woman, you saved my ass and

I thank you

from the bottom of my heart.

Ms. Queen's book, *Real Live Nude Girl*, published in 1997 by Cleis Press, casts resplendent light on the history of sacred Whoredom. Carol Queen reveals that the depravity surrounding

Whoredom is not based on the fact that Whoredom exists, but rather, it is based on the *perception* of Whoredom's existence.

> My "ardent worshippers" and I have no temple today in which to perform a dance that sometimes seems more profane than sacred. In a culture that does not worship the Goddess any longer, these are degenerate times indeed, but not because a once-holy act is still being negotiated in hotel suites, in massage parlors, on city streets. In fact, if prostitution is ever eradicated, it will be a signal that Christianity's murder of Eros is complete, the Goddess's rule completely overturned. Perhaps most prostitutes today are unaware that their profession has a sacred history, and doubtless most clients would define what they do with us as something other than worship. But I believe that an echo of the old relationship, when he was the seeker and she was the Source, are still present when money changes hands today. (Queen, 1997, 190)

It would be *so wonderful* to visit a Sacred Whore temple. Kick down some cash to mix with and undulate in the ol' Goddess's love juices for a while.

Damn, I'm so seethingly jealous of those olden time people.

I daresay the loss of our sacred sexual temples grieves the heart of Carol Queen threefold.

Whoredom has existed, in various guises, for thousands and thousands of years. A main artery of the Goddess's lifeforce, it is too powerful to annihilate.

Whoredom has been successfully vilified.

Whoredom is presently accepted as a very, very bad thing, while its history debases this idea beyond all reckoning.

Sound like any old word that is the title to a book you've been reading lately?

In our present mode of collective consciousness, a Whore is simply a person who exchanges sex for financial resources.

I accept this to be true, but only if it's recognized as one *part* of a much broader cultural-financial order that women participate in for survival. There is no difference between a woman who marries a very powerful man because it is the only way she is guaranteed a "place" in society, and a streetwalker who's never known the illusion of a "guarantee."

Some women opt to be Whores because procuring semen from men's bodies is a bona fide way to make a living in a society where we are viewed as highly expendable citizens.

Ms. Streetwalker exchanges womanly wiles for subsistence.

Some women—such as the late Princess Diana, who once referred to herself as the highest paid prostitute in the world—don't actually *opt* to be Whores, but realize nonetheless that that is exactly what we are.

Ms. Powerwife exchanges womanly wiles for a fancy house in the hills.

In this way of thinking, the issue is *class* rather than Whoredom.

Hugh Grant and Eddie Murphy could lecture on this subject.

Sacred Whore temples flourished in ancient India, the Middle East, Africa, Europe, the Americas and Asia. The word "whore" was a title, used in much the way our word "reverend" is employed today. "Whore" is associated with many words including hus-band, hussy, *puta* (Spanish for "whore"—in Vedic, *puta* means "pure" or "holy"), *ghazye* (Egyptian), *devadasi* (Sanskrit), *horae* (Greek) and *hor* (Hebrew). Whore-priestesses were revered because they taught "a combination of mother-love, tenderness, comfort, mystical enlightenment and sex." (Walker, 1983, 820)

Mary Magdalene was a Whore and Jesus dug her because she taught him the most sacred thing a man can ever hope to learn in his lifetime: how to fuck. Stud that he was, Jesus knew to humble himself to this woman.

I imagine the sex was spectacular.

Let's interpret the notion of Jesus visiting a Whore in a cuntlovin' way. Let's pretend Jesus and his Apostle frat brothers didn't visit Mary Magdalene after a hard night tossing off forty-ouncers and tipping cows in the holy land.

From all the things I've heard about Jesus, he sounds like a pretty decent sort. He looks nice in most of his pictures. You can *tell* Adolph Hitler and George Washington were dickheads just by looking at them. Looking at Jesus, he seems cool. By and large, Jesus evidently had a lot of love and compassion swimming around his heart. He had a pretty huge impact in certain parts of the world, yet left it when he was only thirty-two. You gotta figure Jesus didn't waste a lot of time dinking around. Even if he *did* dink around, he doesn't seem like the kind of guy who'd take an impersonal toss in the hay for a budgeted degree of arousal.

I seriously doubt Jesus perceived Mary Magdalene as any-thing less than an esteemed Teacher. In Jesus' time, Whores were still prophets of sexual power. They taught people how the physical body is a conduit of energy. If Jesus was able to manifest the love in his heart in all the physical actions the bible alleges, Mary Magdalene was certainly one of the people in his life responsible for helping him figure out how to do it.

Though Whores were integral and respected in many times and places, the fear and/or awe of female sexuality certainly rivals Whoredom in age.

I don't know if that big dyke Lilith was a Whore or not, but she was certainly too sexually aggro for Adam and God's liking:

> Hebraic tradition said Adam married Lilith because he grew tired of coupling with beasts, a common custom of Middle-Eastern herdsmen, though the Old Testament declared it a sin (Deuteronomy 27:21). Adam tried to force Lilith to lie beneath him in the "missionary position" favored by male-dominant societies. Moslems were so insistent on the male-superior sexual position that they said, "Accursed be the man who maketh women heaven and himself earth." Catholic authorities said any sexual position other than the male-superior one is sinful. But Lilith was neither a Moslem nor a Catholic. She sneered at Adam's sexual crudity, cursed him, and flew away to make her home by the Red Sea.
>
> God sent angels to fetch Lilith back, but she cursed them too, ignored God's command, and spent her time coupling with "demons" (whose lovemaking evidently pleased her better) and giving birth to a hundred children every day. So God had to produce Eve as Lilith's more

docile replacement. . . . The story of Lilith disappeared from the canonical Bible, but her daughters the *lilim* haunted men for over a thousand years. Well into the Middle Ages, the Jews were still manufacturing amulets to keep away the *lilim*, who were lustful she-demons given to copulating with men in their dreams, causing nocturnal emissions. Naturally, the *lilim* squatted on top of their victims in the position favored by ancient matriarchs. (Walker, 1983, 541-42)

The *lilim* that haunted men in their dreams were manifestations of a growing terror of female sexuality. In our society, this fear has gone past fruition and is presently rotting.

I feel pretty cheated about Whores for a number of reasons:

1. Whores generally subsist within men's domain, under conditions men have formulated for the past odd thousand years, and are largely inaccessible to women.

2. Most Whores are completely unaware of how important they are to society, and subsequently do not have the opportunity to learn how to be all-compassionate, all-loving, all-giving and all-receiving incarnations of the Goddess.

3. I've never been with a Whore because any Whore who knows she's one of the Goddess's priestesses would cost my entire disposable income for six months.

I do, however, have a frame of reference because I know what it is like to be in the arms of the Goddess.

One time I got blessed by this Goddess incarnation named Ammachi. She's not a Whore, but she's by far the closest personification of an olden time sacred temple priestess I've ever personally encountered.

Ammachi is a woman from India who comes to America and has these ashram things. The first time I went to her ashram thing, I had no idea what it was about. I saw a bunch of mostly white people dressed in white clothes who bugged me with their "Oh, I am so very holy and drink herbal tea constantly" vibration.

But the music was amazing.

Ammachi sat in the front of the room on a bunch of pillows. Musicians, attendants, children and flowers surrounded her. Thousands of flowers, like when Princess Diana died. She sat there with her eyes closed, and chanted. Probably, she was meditating. Wearing a flowing white sari, she was covered with chiffon, silk, everything soft and whispery. I figured she understood the concept of an ashram far better than I, so I did the same as her. Closed my eyes, sat and listened.

This lasted a long time, but like in a dream, I don't know how many minutes and hours passed.

Then there were the rustling sounds of people standing up. I opened my eyes. Everyone was forming a double-file line that led to Ammachi.

My friends told me she was gonna bless people, so we queued up. The line was very, very long, snaking throughout the entire large building we were in. If it had been a line at the post office that I *absolutely had to stand in* for some reason or another, I woulda sold my soul to the person in front to give me cuts. But this line was different. The music and nice quiet felt good. Being blessed by an incarnation of the Goddess is also much more alluring than overnighting IRS forms.

Before I knew it, I was next.

An attendant led me to her and kinda helped me kneel down right. Ammachi seized me gently—if you can imagine that—and pulled me into her lap. She cradled me, murmuring sweet chanting sounds into my ear. Her body engulfed mine and I relaxed—almost melted—into her. My face buried in her shoulder and neck, I breathed in her smell.

This is when I really, truly started to freak on the wonder of Ammachi. After holding hundreds of people in this manner, you would think she'd start to kinda stink. I was nowhere near the beginning of the line. The sun set and went down, down, down to Australia while I stood in that line. A lot of people were in her arms before me, but the woman smelled like flowers. Not perfumey at all. Like if you covered every inch of your bedroom floor with freshly cut bouquets of jasmine, gardenia, roses, hyacinth, carnations, sweet peas and freesia is what she smelled like. And this smell wasn't coming from the flowers around her, it exuded from her skin, the fabrics of her sari and veils. It filled my whole body, permeated my pores. Her smell made me so giddy the attendant had to help me stand back up again. She stared deeply into my eyes and pressed flower petals and chocolate kisses into my hand.

I stumbled away like a drunk.

Like I just had one 'dem orgasms to raise the dead.

Lordisa.

For a whole week afterwards, my entire apartment smelled

like Ammachi. Everywhere I went, I smelled her smell. Walking down the street with one of my friends, the smell of Ammachi would assail me. I'd go, "*Damn*, do you smell that?" And my friend'd go, "Car exhaust? What?"

As Ammachi's smell faded from my life, I started thinking about what happened when she blessed me.

It was the first time in my life I felt *loved*. Physically, emotionally, psychically, spiritually, *deeply loved* from the epidermis of my skin that featured a couple of ugly zits, to the core of my heart that is still traumatized by the death of my brother, abortions, meanspirited lovergirls and other nasty hurts. It is a consciousness-broadening freak-out to feel love in this way.

"What," I wondered, "is the difference between Ammachi and a Whore?" Ammachi gave me unconditional love, no questions asked. She healed me and helped me understand more about love. I was one of many people cradled in her embrace that day. Ammachi needs money to keep spreading her love, and I bought plenty of Ammachi paraphernalia to support her.

She doesn't offer erotic love to people, but any cuntlovin' Whore will tell ya, eroticism is a *part* of sexual love.

After Ammachi blessed me, after her flower smell took over my life for a week, after I sat down and thought about it long and hard, I realized her gift. She clues people in on what love really, really is. That way, it's easier to know what love really, really isn't. She helps people identify love, so we can call it into our lives. In the grand panorama of my life, I was in Ammachi's world, in Ammachi's arms, for mere moments.

Those moments changed me forever.

This is some serious-assed power founded in cuntlove.

The nemesis of this power is sexual cuntfear. One of the many, many, many casualties of our culture's negative sexual fear sits in a jail cell awaiting execution as you read this.

Aileen Wuornos is an ex-Whore on death row in Florida. She murdered seven men. She is the only "serial killer" ever to plead self-defense.

Not long after Ms. Wuornos walked through the prison doors, I attended Diamanda Galás's performance of a vocal composition entitled *Shrei X*. Ms. Galás's three-and-a-half octave range left me reeling in pain. Her haunting, stunning presence shattered all my fear.

I interviewed her the next day and asked, "What inspired *Shrei X?*"

Well, one thing was Aileen Wuornos. It's a long story. There's a documentary out called *The Selling of A Serial Killer* about Aileen Wuornos. It's a very, very interesting movie. She's a real hero of mine because without taking a predatory stance, you're fucked. In her case, literally.

If you're a prostitute and somebody rapes you, it's just fucken a shitty feeling. Aileen would go through the sex part and then the John would want to do something else, like fuck her up the ass and put alcohol up her ass. She got to where she went over the edge and said, "No more." She reached Critical Mass, said *No,* and started killing people who were abusing her. And because she was seen as being

c
u
n
t

predatory, she got the death penalty. She's not seen as somebody who has the law on her side for the job that she was doing. A job that is, very effectively, if not legalized, condoned, as long as she pays out the cops. She didn't *have* any protection and it got to where she had to protect herself. So she protected herself and went to prison. As a woman, she's obviously powerless, but she's *really* powerless. A lesbian prostitute is seen as totally powerless trash.

The silence at the end of *Shrei X* is the silence that her dumbfuck lawyers sang to her because she was found guilty. Guilty, guilty, guilty.

Because Ms. Wuornos is perceived as being "totally powerless trash," because Ms. Wuornos resides in an exceptionally cuntfearing society and because Ms. Wuornos's case yielded quite a bit of media interest, her "lawyer" seems to have come to the conclusion that he could make a pretty penny selling her "story." *Especially* if his client is put to death. After watching *Aileen Wuornos: The Selling of a Serial Killer*, one is rather confronted with the idea that the people who one would traditionally expect to support Ms. Wuornos—namely her attorneys—are plainly itching for her to be executed as a ferocious serial killer.

Which she is not.

Aileen Wuornos is an economically challenged woman who defended herself and needs a decent, intelligent lawyer to get her the fuck out of jail.

If I may be so bold, I would like to dedicate a portion of Kinnie
Starr's song "Buttons" to every Whore who suffers under the
influence of our sexually retarded, destructive culture:

> and we could call it out when it doesn't suit us both 'cause
> there's a magnitude of choices and a really big boat
> and that big boat floats on a restless ocean
> singing about the chances of protective devotion
>
> for the girlfriend who stands on a street waiting on a trick
> some man demands that she lift her skirt quick
> she's got a mother, a daughter and a lover
> you tell me why she shouldn't have safe cover
>
> 'cause if the laws made sense
> she would have a legal fence
> to keep her clientele clean
> and she could still pay the rent
> she's got a mother, a daughter and a lover
> you tell me why she shouldn't have safe cover

A few years ago a friend of mine was twenty-five cents short for
bus fare. None of us had change either. She turned to a gentleman at the bus stop and asked if he could spare a quarter. He
responded, *"What?* What *you* askin' me for a quarter for? Girl,
you got a *goldmine* between your legs."

This sentence rang in my ears for years.

Cuntlovingly decontextualized, "a goldmine between your legs" is a wonderful sentiment. Like what you find at the end of the rainbow. The idea of women having a goldmine between our legs was so appealing to me, I wrote a little blues song about it:

you gotts a goldmine between your legs,
a goldmine between your legs,
no need to be poor in the u.s.a.
you gotts a goldmine between your legs.
honey why you givin' it away?
we all know them boys'll pay
equal pay for equal labor,
not only love but charge your neighbor.
no need to be poor in the u.s.a.
you gotts a goldmine between your legs.
my momma's broke and all alone
even though she made me a home.
if only she'd charged dear old dad
momma'd be drivin' a shiny jag.
no need to be poor in the u.s.a.
you gotts a goldmine between your legs
does hubby make more money, honey?
wouldn't it be really funny
if he didn't get no fine puss-say
unless he lined your coffers, hey hey.
you gotts a goldmine between your legs,
goldmine between your legs,
no need to be poor in the u.s.a.
you gotts a goldmine between your legs.

All ladies have the power to cash in on the goldmine between our legs. Not necessarily with the objective of financial security or spiritual fulfillment, but for the most important reasons of all: future generations and our cuntlovin' selves.

On a less metaphorical level, nothing but good and fabulousness would come from erecting temples in honor of women's sexuality, filled with women and women-trained male Whores who offered us lessons in how to love and be loved.

Whores were in business back before the Red Sea ever thought about parting. Whores have no labor unions, no health insurance, no retirement fund, no unemployment insurance and no legal rights. Since a chain is only as strong as its weakest link, the nonexistent rights and freedoms of women who understand the power of cunts conceivably more than any other group of women in our society bespeaks the constitution of the chain we ladies are dealing with here.

Is it a mere coincidence that women so specifically, physically associated with cunts have no rights in this culture?

Get out.

Without honoring Whores, we cannot truly understand and transcend the dynamics of violence, destruction and ignorance fostered in our cuntfearing society. The fact that some women are considered "bad" is a puritanically based value judgement that reinforces a fatal division between women. Many women allow our lives and sexual expression to be dictated by the threat of being perceived as "Whores." Because of thinking like this, our society is brimming with women who have a hard time understanding, for instance, that

Whores *can be and are* sexually assaulted.

"How," one might ask, "can a woman who accepts money for sex *be* raped?" Or perhaps, "What does a woman who puts herself in that position *expect?*"

The fact that either question is considered *at all plausible* reflects the self-defeating ignorance we ourselves perpetuate.

The measure of respect Whores receive is in direct proportion to the measure of respect all women receive. Until there is an established, respected place for Whores is this society, no woman will have an established, respected foundation of power.

There is no circumventing this.

Until there is a shift in consciousness about the potential of Whores, we will continue to live in a society which offers no formally acknowledged Teachers to awaken us to our power as sexual beings.

Ain't no getting 'round this one either.

The fact that Whores are no longer exalted and respected is very much a reflection of our culture's collective sexual retardation and fear of women's innate sexual power.

The aptly named Carol Queen is my personal prophet on Whoredom's future in our society.

To guide another person to orgasm, to hold and caress, to provide companionship and initiation to new forms of sex, to embody the Divine and embrace the seeker—these are healing and holy acts. Every prostitute can do these things, whether or not s/he understands their spiritual potential. For us to see ourselves as sacred whores, for our clients to acknowledge the many facets of desire they bring to us, can be a powerful shift in consciousness. We show the face of the Goddess in a culture that has tried for millennia to break and denigrate Her, just as some today claim *we* are broken and denigrated. They are not correct, and the Goddess will not be broken. In our collective extraordinary experience we prostitutes have healed even those who do not honor us. Were the attack on us over, we could begin to heal the whole world.

After seven thousand years of oppression, I declare this the time to bring back our temple. (Queen, 1997, 204-5)

Whoredom is a constant.

Perception fluctuates evermore.

I don't know about you, but I like the idea of respecting things that have been around a lot longer than me. I drive old cars and live in old houses. I gravitate towards old souls and listen to what old folks say. My favorite games—chess and backgammon—are old, old, old.

So you see, if I were to find Whoredom and the Perception Surrounding Whoredom at a garage sale, I'd definitely buy the Whoredom.

Even if it was dented up, needed a new paint job and cost a coupla bucks more.

Orgasms from Cunts

Thanks to the perception surrounding Whoredom in our
culture, no one teaches us how to fuck. We grow up
and either figure it out for ourselves or settle into
some habitual bog of sexual expression.
Whatever.
Sexual expression must be made manifest in
the physical world, *somehow*. Since it cannot be
completely repressed, people sometimes hide stuff
and get into weird things like eating shit. Sexual expression is a
current of kinetic energy running through our bodies. It
whirligigs up our cunts, charges through our entire being and
slam dances on out into the world back through our cunts.

Comin' our brains out.

Sometimes we holler 'n shake the windows in their panes.

Our cunts are powerhouses.

Cuntlovin' women who make the conscious decision to
oversee the smooth operation of our powerhouses know all this.

One of my prized possessions is my 1965 Random House
Dictionary. It lived in my parent's house before I. Though

technically it belonged to everyone, I took it with me when I moved away. No one complained. Ever since I could read, that dictionary and I were inseparable.

When I was ten, I invited a boy I liked very much over to our house. We hung out in my room, mooning over each other and listening to records, until my father opened the door. He told the boy to go home and steered me by the elbow into the kitchen. There, at the table sat my mother and my dear friend, the Random House Dictionary. I sensed I was in deep shit, but didn't know why. Mom had a serious look on her face and Dad seemed kinda pissed.

He said, "Look up the word 'reputation' and read it aloud."

My father, the devout atheist with the photographic memory who knew the Encyclopedia Britannica by heart, had us quote from the dictionary in much the same manner as children in other families were required to quote from the Holy Book.

I read the definition for "reputation":

rep-u-ta-tion (rep ye ta shen), n. 1. the estimation in which a person or thing is held, esp. by the community or the public generally: *a man of good reputation.* 2. favorable repute; good name: *to ruin one's reputation by misconduct.* 3. a favorable and publicly recognized name or standing for merit, achievement, etc.: *to build up a reputation.* 4. the estimation or name of being, having, having done, etc., something specified: *He has the reputation of being a shrewd businessman.*

the anatomical jewel

I was thoroughly mystified, but after reading the definition of "reputation," I felt decidedly ashamed.

Dirty.

My dad looked at me sternly and said, "You must *never* have boys in your room with the door closed."

"But we were listening to records," I argued. "I always close the door when my friends come over and we listen to records."

Mom: "Inga, it's very important not to get a bad reputation. Letting boys in your room and closing the door is one way to get a bad reputation."

Dad: "When your girlfriends come over, you can close the door, but when boys come over, keep it open."

Little did my parents know, it was me and my *girl* friends who engaged in sexual activity. At age ten, I'd *remotely* entertained the notion of kissing boys, while at least three of my girlfriends and I had figured out how to make each other come by the time we were seven.

I've had the satisfaction of clueing my mom in, but I wish my dad were alive so I could say, "Yo, Pops, if you were *really* concerned with my chastity, you shouldn't have let certain friends spend the night with me, ya fool."

This isn't to preface my anger towards my parents for instilling in me shameful associations about my budding sexuality.

They Did the Best They Could.

I quelled any animosity I may have felt towards them the time I saw this real old Japanese print of two people having rapturous sex while their three children peacefully played a game with marbles at their feet. It is the epitome of the family-at-home-together picture. The kids don't care that the parents are fucking because fucking is as much a part of life as playing with marbles. They are completely unconcerned with what their parents are doing because *it's no big deal.* They're just fucking. The parents are playing a game that somebody taught them how to play. By the time those kids got big, they'd know fucking like they knew the soft, glassy chink of marbles colliding.

This was not my reality.

When my mother was pregnant with Nick, the youngest of her brood, she described how sexual intercourse created the magic of a baby in her belly.

"You and Dad have done that *four times?*" I asked, thoroughly disgusted.

People helped me out when it was time for me to walk and ride a two-wheeler. Everyone I knew encouraged me to talk, use the toilet, sing, draw, swim, read, write and make lots of friends.

I am very fortunate and grateful that I got helped out quite a bit.

There was this one—rather crucial—part of my being, however, that was pretty much left to the elements. I didn't get nearly as much encouragement learning how to express myself sexually as I did learning how to pronounce big words.

When I became sexually active with men, sex wasn't what I wanted *at all.* I wanted love and affection. I had fun having sex with my girlfriends, but it was just that: fun. Suddenly, it seems one day, I was supposed to re-enact this with boys and it just wasn't the same, spontaneous, jiveass, wanton fun. It's quite the bummer—not to mention life-threatening reality—that I didn't figure this out 'til after I'd tested sheets with surfers, vatos, punks, nerds and a rather sadistic wrestler-chiropractor.

I didn't even really think about my formal, heterosexual awakening until years after the fact, when two of my hometown friends and I talked about it.

Why did we fuck those boys who never exactly made our clits pound out the Bohemian Rhapsody in the first place? What were we doing? Did we love ourselves at all? We certainly mustn't have, or we would *at the very least,* have practiced safe sex. Why didn't we understand that our quest for love and affection could have easily killed us, and why didn't it? Was the Goddess magnanimously smiling upon the truly ignorant?

Toni Childs sings this really cool song I wish I had heard when I was seventeen. It's called "I Just Want Affection," and it's one of many beautiful songs on the album *The Woman's Boat.* This song taught me about the difference between erotic closeness and fucking.

Lots of girls grow up thinking the way to be loved is to fuck because our culture holds that affection is part and parcel to gettin' down. But in my mind, and in the minds of many, many cuntlovin' women I know, it is dimly related, but not the same thing at all.

Had I been left to my innate feminine wiles, I would've found a much safer and supportive way to procure affection, love and acceptance, starting with myself.

The happy ending is, though, that through trial, error, forgiveness and willingness to accept my ignorance, I learned that I'm the Cuntlovin' Ruler of My Sexual Universe.

Which leads to the story of Mademoiselle Precious, my cousin's daughter.

When Mademoiselle was seven, her parents granted her a premier waltz with independence: a visit to the city to stay with my musical concubine and me for a week one summer.

We were a little nervous. Neither of us had been around kids for long, parentless durations of time. Our home was not designed around the premise of a child's entertainment requirements. We didn't even have a television set. What if she was bored with our lives?

But we needn't have worried. Mlle. Precious loved all our friends. She loved going to the coffee shops, the river, everywhere we took her. She loved the Free Box in our apartment building and insisted on visiting it first thing every morning.

We all got along quite famously.

One day, my musical concubine said, "I've seen Mlle. Precious jiggling under her covers on the couch. Do you think her parents have talked to her about masturbating?"

I said I didn't know.

"Do you think you should talk to her about masturbating?"

I thought about how embarrassed I was that time my sister barged into the bathroom while I was whacking off with the shower massage. I also thought about how I probably wouldn't have had such a baggage-load of negative beliefs to dispell as an adult if just *one measly person* had told me it was fine and dandy to bandy my clit when I was a kid.

But, *jeez,* talking to Mlle. Precious about masturbating? What if it embarrassed her? What if it scarred her for life and it would be all my fault? What would I say?

I said I didn't know again.

It was quite the preoccupational quandary in my mind all day long.

We went to the river, played in the mud and the water.

When we came home, my musical concubine made phone calls and Mlle. Precious and I took a bubble bath. We were busy getting clean and shiny and suddenly, it just jumped out of me.

I said, "Hey, Precious. I don't know if you ever do, but if you ever play with your wahchee (that's what her family calls cunts), I just want you to know it's okay."

She turned crimson, looked at me and then down at the water. "I don't do that. I don't play with my wahchee."

Shit.

Goddamn.

I spluttered, "I *know.* I mean, it doesn't matter. I just wanted to tell you that *if* you ever *did,* it's all right. Everybody plays with their wahchee, I swear to god."

She glared at me. "Well, *I* don't."

I hastily changed the subject and we splashed more bubbles to life.

After a few minutes, Mlle. Precious says, "Everybody plays with their wahchee?"

My heart leaped in my chest. Oh, how I smiled inside.

"Yeah. Everybody."

"Do you?"

"Yup."

"Does your musical concubine?"

"Yeah."

"My mom?"

"Probably. I mean, I would *imagine*. Just about everybody does, Precious. And it's *perfectly fine* if you do, too. Even if people tell you it's bad, they're just scared or stupid. It's not bad at all and *everybody* plays with their wahchee."

She laughed crazy, absolutely thrilled, and yelled, "Everybody plays with their wahchee?"

I screamed, "Everybody plays with their wahchee!"

We chanted, yelling at the top of our lungs, "Ev-ree-body plays with their wahh-chee! Ev-ree-body plays with their wahh-chee! Ev-ree-body plays with their wahh-chee!"

My musical concubine, still on the phone: "Jesus Christ! What are you two screaming about? What the hell's a wahchee?"

We laughed and splashed and chanted and flooded the whole bathroom.

I hope this experience has a positive effect on Mademoiselle Precious's sexuality. I hope she remembers all her life that there's not a problem in the world with her jilling off. However, even if our conversation gets lost in her shuffle of growing up, our little talk heartened *me* tremendously. I felt like I'd righted an inadvertent wrong committed against me when I was a little girl.

Felt the cards of karma riffle into place.

In my cosmology, Wilhelm Reich holds the distinction of being the only male psychoanalyst who could knock on my door and be invited in for tea.

Reich's books were banned in America for many years, while he himself was ostracized—even imprisoned—by the U.S. government during McCarthy's scary reign.

He challenged the puritanical ideas about sexuality in our

culture. In laywoman terms, Reich believed humans store emotions in our muscles. During orgasm, muscles in the body contract, then relax, thus releasing emotions. Reich asserted that all aspects of healthy human psychology are dependent upon one's sexual expression.

When you cry, laugh or feel free as a bird after coming, it is partly because you just released a bunch of yucky crap that's been building up inside your body for days, months, years, possibly your entire lifetime.

A moment of epiphany on this subject occurred after six months of Reichian therapy. I was at the beach, thinking and watching the waves. The revelation assailed me quite suddenly, as revelations are wont to do: Each wave is an orgasm. Sometimes they're big. Sometimes they're small. Sometimes they tear faces of cliff from the earth's surface. If the ocean did not have waves, it would be a big, salty lake. A lake is a still pool of water. Personally, I don't venture into water that doesn't move. Bored, malevolent monsters live in bodies of water that do not move.

When women function like the ocean, we live happy, healthy lives. Holding on to stuff that does not serve us in our present situation creates actual, physical blockages within our bodies.

Bored, malevolent monsters.

Which, on the individual level, manifest in bitterness, stifled creativity, sexual perversion and unwillingness to trust, love and/or touch.

Collectively—when an entire society is sexually repressed— phenomena such as war, rape, racism, greed and wholesale shitty behavior are considered acceptable.

It is difficult to strip away cultural thought-patterns and stereo-types to arrive at the pulsating naked core of Woman: Cuntlovin' Fucklove Prophetess. I realized the enormity of this very task on New Year's Day in 1995.

I was walking down the street when a gentleman whose family and tribe have lived in the Pacific Northwest for thou-sands of years asked me for some spare change.

Due to the rising cost of living, I don't believe in spare change. As I handed him a dollar, he peered into my eyes and smiling, asked, "Hey, did you get Any for New Year's?"

I was just about to say, "That's none of your fucking business, dickhead," but his eyeballs caught me off guard. He didn't have perving eyeballs. He had very nice, open eyeballs with a pretty glint in them. He was just good-naturedly asking me if I rang in the new year with a celebratory tumble in the sack. And, as it happened, I actually did ring in the new year in just such a manner.

So I said, "Yeah."

The gentleman positively *beamed*. He said, "Hey! Me too! Ain't nothin' like gettin' Some on New Year's to humble ya, know what I mean?"

As I walked home, I thought about this man and his message. I thought, sex truly is humbling. I thought, sex, birth, life and death are all humbling. Most of all, I thought how thankful I was to this gentleman for giving me a beautiful message about sex, something seldom resonated in society. I tried to think of all the positive, reinforcing messages about sex

I have access to on a general basis whenever I leave my home, or otherwise subject myself to this culture.

The only one I readily managed to summon was the words of a very nice Lummi gentleman on New Year's Day in 1995.

All my life, I've absorbed stimuli about sex from my culture, family, friends and teachers. Most of this information has been hopelessly gnarled all up with violence, racism, power, purity, shame, denial, guilt, humiliation, victimization, objectification, rejection and unimaginative stereotypes of sexual identity.

Probably even more stuff than that.

It all, all, all, all, all, all, all, all, all stems from fear of women and our enormous sexual power.

When we were children, one of my older brother's favorite means of torment was to sit down near me, cut a *foul*, noiseless fart and wait. As soon as he ascertained that I'd detected his gastric horror, he'd restrain my hands so I could neither run nor cover my nose, and diabolically whisper, "Silence is deadly."

While his farts miraculously never threatened my life, I agree with this sentiment wholeheartedly.

Since the early days of the church, women had been barred from speaking in the house of God as well as preaching, teaching, or speaking in public: "As in all the churches of the saints," wrote St. Paul, "wives should keep silence in the churches. They are not permitted to speak, but should be subordinate, as even the law says. If there is anything they desire to know, let them ask their husbands at home. For it is shameful for a woman to speak in church." This prohibition grew out of the synthesis of separate traditions, the Greek, which taught that women were by nature inferior to men and therefore should be their subordinates, and the Biblical, which suggested to many readers that women be perpetually silent as a punishment for the sins of Eve, whose garrulousness brought disaster to all mankind: "The curse of God pronounced on your sex weighs still on the world. Guilty you must bear its hardships," wrote Tertullian in the third century, "You are the devil's gateway . . . you softened up with your cajoling words the man against whom the devil could not prevail by force." Over the centuries these themes hardened until silence became a virtue particularly recommended to women. "By silence, indeed, women achieve the fame of eloquence," wrote one Renaissance commentator. (Brown, 1986, 59)

The enforced silence of women allows men's fear of us and our sexual power to reign unchallenged. Thus the wisdom of brilliant people such as Audre Lorde is not venerated, and we are still sent to schools where idiotic puds like Aristotle are worshipped.

A-hem:

Just as it sometimes happens that deformed offspring are produced by deformed parents, and sometimes not, so the offspring produced by a female are sometimes female, sometimes not, but male. The reason is that the female is as it were a deformed male; and the menstrual charge is semen, though . . . it lacks one constituent, and only one,

the principle of Soul. . . . Thus the physical part, the body,
comes from the female, and the Soul from the male, since
the Soul is the essence of a particular body. . . . females are
weaker and colder in their nature, and we should look
upon the female state as being as it were a deformity,
though one which occurs in the ordinary course of nature.
(Aristotle, as quoted in Brown, 1986, 188)

To the best of my knowledge, it wasn't until 1968 when Valerie
Solanas published her *S.C.U.M. Manifesto,* that this particular form
of intolerance was duplicated with any serious eloquence:

It is now technically possible to reproduce without the aid of
males (or, for that matter, females) and to produce only
females. We must begin immediately to do so. Retaining the
male has not even the dubious purpose of reproduction. The
male is a biological accident: the y (male) gene is an
incomplete x (female) gene, that is, has an incomplete set of
chromosomes. In other words, the male is an incomplete
female, a walking abortion, aborted at the gene stage. To be
male is to be deficient, emotionally limited; maleness is a
deficiency disease and males are emotional cripples.

The male is completely egocentric, trapped inside
himself, incapable of empathizing or identifying with
others, of love, friendship, affection or tenderness. He is a
completely isolated unit, incapable of rapport with
anyone. His responses are entirely visceral, not cerebral;
his intelligence is a mere tool in the service of his drives
and needs, he is incapable of mental passion, mental

interaction; he can't relate to anything other than his own physical sensations. He is a half dead, unresponsive lump, incapable of giving or receiving pleasure or happiness; consequently, he is at best an utter bore, an inoffensive blob, since only those capable of absorption in others can be charming. He is trapped in a twilight zone halfway between humans and apes, and is far worse off than apes because, unlike the apes, he is capable of a large array of negative feelings—hate, jealousy, contempt, disgust, guilt, shame, doubt—and moreover he is *aware* of what he is and isn't.

While Aristotle is lauded in our culture, Valerie Solanas is considered—when she's considered at all—to be a terribly unhinged individual who died homeless on the streets of San Francisco in 1988. Whereas, if you changed the pronouns throughout her manifesto, and backdated it a couple of decades, you'd probably have the ramblings of a brilliant, Pulitzer Prize–winning male scholar.

See how that works?

Women and silence have been historically mashed together like potatoes and cheese. Our true erotic nature is not exalted. Rather, it is mutated into some manageable illusion created and sustained by men. Meanwhile, the Washington Monument alone attests to the grandeur with which male erotic nature is glorified.

This same pattern is found in the scant funding for both breast cancer research and the risk of female-to-female transmission of the HIV virus, versus the gazillions of dollars poured into research for prostate cancer, and the risk of male-to-male transmission of the HIV virus.

In an interview in *Bust* #10, the beautiful, genius porn star, Nina Hartley describes what's at stake here.

> I got the first edition of *Our Bodies, Ourselves* for my 13th brithday and it was the most powerful book I'd ever read next to *Sex for One*, which saved my life. Sex is enlightening. The reality is that once a woman knows that the pleasure goddess is at the end of her arm, then she can swing her hand in front of her crotch anytime and woops! there it is, anytime she wants. It's really easy—let's see: teddy bears, washing machines, jacuzzi jets, vibrators, cunnilingus, fucking, ooo, lots of things can do it. Women are denied pleasure because pleasure is very, very powerful, very, very potent. (93)

Women reach orgasm via our clitoris, through contractions of the muscles deep within our cunts or by stimulation of our G-spots. Sometimes all three, or any combination. Women ejaculate. Fingers or other apparati strategically placed up a woman's ass can lead to ten-minute-long multiple orgasms. Women can come just by looking at—or imagining—some major turn-on for a while. Women can come over and over, one orgasm right after the last. Women have orgasms in many, many different ways.

Men, on the other hand, come when their cock is stroked, via a hand, mouth, cunt or anus. Many men can also achieve orgasm through stimulation of their prostate gland, via their asshole. Sadly though, the general feeling among straight men is, "I ain't no fucking faggot, so keep clear of my ass." Thus, a lot of men deprive themselves of this (I've gathered) highly pleasurable sensation.

After a man comes, he's usually spent for at least fifteen minutes, and generally, that's it for the session. This, of course, is in the event that he has not studied any Tantric-type breathing and muscle control practices, which the vast majority of men in our culture don't have the opportunity, inclination or self-discipline to explore.

As a dick is a finite structure, with a visible beginning and end, so too is the potential for a male orgasm.

As a cunt is infinite—how many bloody mysteries and future generations are hiding up there, somewhere?—so too is the potential for female orgasm.

I'm setting my imagination free to roam here, but if I were a man, and had no *biological* idea what it was like to have such a complex orgasm mechanism as a cunt—with *so many* intricate, endless and fascinating possibilities for achieving pleasure—I'd be pretty nervous making love to a woman. And I might find millions and billions of ways to camouflage my nervousness, rather than be like Jesus and just humble myself.

Aristotle opted to obsessively devote his life to the creation of an elaborate belief system based on total cuntfear, rather than simply face reality. That seems like pretty nervous behavior to me. Ditto Sigmund Freud--the Rush Limbaugh our society actually takes seriously.

You might as well throw pretty much all male politicians, military leaders, industrial revolution kings, mafia dons, bankers, artists and executives in there too.

After all, if Rockefeller, for instance, knew how to please a woman, he'd hardly have transferred so much nervous sexual energy to proving his virility—in the guise of Standard Oil—to every woman, child and man on the planet.

In this culture we preserved the words, laws, codices, artwork, religions, music and mergers of a bunch of nervous, insecure lovers. Evidently, there is no shortage of them. Then we went and hailed them as Geniuses of Our Time.

Men have gone to exorbitant lengths to camouflage—rather than reckon with—their cuntfear for thousands of years. The naked female form is idolized, obsessed over and blamed for any maltreatment it meets. There is a veritable surplus of references that state how sinful, impossible, miraculous or wrong it is for women to experience sexual pleasure.

Retarded male sexual power is expressed in maneuvers people have come to look upon with unerring respect, such as warring, ruling or becoming heads of production companies in Hollywood.

In offense to women who positively *refuse* to remain silent, some women are placed on pedestals in poses of righteousness for holding our tongues (no pun intended) in religious, political, artistic, economic and legal arenas. The women on the pedestals, then, provide a twofold service: a) presenting physical evidence that men have no interest in holding us down, and b) serving as a point of reference for other women who want to be "heard" in this society.

This isn't to say there aren't countless numbers of women fighting our hearts raw in all of the aforementioned arenas. If we're vocally pro-woman or speak in favor of healthy human sexuality, our silencing (i.e., the end of our careers, à la the brilliant, courageous, stunning Dr. Jocelyn Elders) is imminent.

Since we are invalidated for speaking our truth, or worse, mute from the get go, men never face how amazing our cunts are, and further, never reckon with the infernal jealousy they have that we can come in so many ways, so many times in succession.

> We young women of Arabia recognized that the men of our land would never pursue social change for our sex, that we would have to force change. As long as Saudi women accepted their authority, men would rule. We surmised that it was the responsibility of each individual woman to ferment desire for control of her life and other female lives within her small circle. Our women are so beaten down by centuries of mistreatment that our movement had to begin with an awakening of the spirit. (Sasson, 1992, 75-6)

Things *are* gonna change, and cuntlovin' ladies all over the world *are* gonna make it happen. Just as soon as we accept the fact that our cunts are the Holiest of Grails, the Hopefulest of Diamonds, the Goldenest of Medals.

Claire Cavanah is one of the owners of Toys in Babeland, a woman-positive sex paraphernalia/erotic multi-media store with branches in Seattle, Washington, and New York City. I interviewed her about women's fears of our own sexuality:

> A lot of straight men come into the store because their partners won't come with them. I guess a lot of women can't imagine a place where there's so much freedom and peace involved with finding out what they want and then getting it. Getting what you want sexually is a huge achievement, and it seems to frighten a lot of women.

They're afraid that if they see how much fun and pleasure they can experience by incorporating a vibrator or dildo into their sexual activities, they won't need their partner anymore. They're afraid to be free. It seems many people have this weird desire to *settle*. It's hard to keep growing, to constantly find out more. For some women, the desire to grow stops even before they learn how to come.

Obstacles such as these would not exist in a society that required students to read Audre Lorde's "Uses of the Erotic: The Erotic as Power" in high school.

The erotic is a measure between the beginnings of our sense of self and the chaos of our strongest feelings. It is an internal sense of satisfaction to which, once we have experienced it, we know we can aspire. For having experienced the fullness of this depth of feeling and recognizing its power, in honor and self-respect we can require no less of ourselves.

It is never easy to demand the most from ourselves, from our lives, from our work. To go beyond the encouraged mediocrity of our society is to encourage excellence. But giving in to the fear of feeling and working to capacity is a luxury only the unintentional can afford, and the unintentional are those who do not wish to guide their own destinies. (Lorde, 1984, 54)

Let's, shall we, go ahead, drop all the bullshit and get down to the nitty-gritty reality that you and your cunt are the Cuntlovin' Rulers of Your Sexual Universe.

Because I have no idea what turns you on, what (if any) sexual hang-ups and/or fetishes you may have, whether you come via penetration, clitoral stimulation, a G-spot massage or by tickling your bellybutton at 1:18 p.m. with a redorangeyellow sunset rose in full bloom, I'm gonna skip all the guesswork and go right to sources. You answer all your own questions, make all your own guesses and explore your own sexual expression.

If you have a really hard time letting go of cultural mindsets you have learned about sex, I highly suggest opening up a dialogue with your women friends or family members. Find out what the women in your immediate community have been taught and how they process and deal with negative shit. Refrain from focusing conversation on your *lover(s)*. Keep everything real nice and personal.

I could underscore the point until profits from the feminine hygiene industry were placed in a college fund for young women and *still*, I don't think I'd do justice to precisely how *profoundly* exchanging stories, fantasies and problems with women has improved the quality of my life.

I know of seven absolutely woman-positive sex stores in America. A woman-positive sex store is *not* a porno shack with twenty-five-cent semen-encrusted peep booths in the back.

I've been in three of the seven: Toys in Babeland in Seattle, Good Vibrations in San Francisco and It's My Pleasure in Portland. All three are owned by women who are *fucken full on dedicated* to redressing sexual stereotypes that keep women down. The atmosphere in each of these stores is: "Come on in

123

and browse at your leisure, ask questions, take a vibrator for a test drive in our private boudoir. Most importantly, enjoy yourself." All three are stocked with state-of-the-art sexual apparati, beautiful, informative and erotic books, videos, calendars, comics, photo-journals. Every staff member is patient, sensitive and totally helpful. *The women who work at these stores are hired for their ability to be fully supportive to women who manage to shove aside their embarrassment and shame to ask, "Where the fuck is my G-spot and why should I care?"*

The four remaining stores are Eve's Garden and Toys in Babeland in New York City, A Woman's Touch in Madison, Wisconsin, and Grand Opening in Brookline, Massachusetts. Claire Cavanah told me about these stores, and since she and co-owner Rachel Venning are double-handedly responsible for providing many, many women in their community with information and the means to come our brains out, even though I haven't physically investigated these stores, I'm willing to wager they're equally cool.

That covers the Midwest and the east and west coasts. Pile all your girlfriends into a car and barrel ass to one of these stores. Plan a trip! Whee! Spend the weekend contemplating, discovering and achieving your orgasmic potential.

What's that you say? You live in Kansas? You're tied to a job in Tennessee? Well, these ladies got you covered, too. All six stores have mail-order catalogs and/or websites.

The women who work at these stores are warriors in their own right, and have dedicated themselves to freeing women's sexual, erotic nature.

They love you!

They want you to come and come and come.

Write or call and order a catalog. Phone numbers and addresses are listed in the Cuntlovin' Guide to the Universe at the end of this book.

A number of exceptional books and videos are available. They teach everything you could ever want to know about vibrators, dildos, G-spots, female ejaculation, eroticism, Kegel exercises, Ben Wa balls, butt plugs, S&M, pubococcygeal muscles, the clitoris, female erogenous zones and the supportive culture of expressive female sexuality. Some of the more immutably germane include:

Books

A New View of a Woman's Body: A Fully Illustrated Guide [ISBN 0-9629945-0-2], by the Federation of Feminist Women's Health Centers, illustrated by Suzann Gage, photos by Sylvia Morales, Feminist Health Press, 8420 Santa Monica Blvd., Los Angeles, CA 90046, (213) 650-1508. This book is *invaluable*. Did you hear me? *Priceless. You must have this book.* It includes not only a complete list of every woman-positive health center in the country, an awesome glossary, a reference bibliography and breathtaking illustrations and photographs, but it covers every aspect of cunt care imaginable. Explicit descriptions of self-exams, reproductive anatomy, analytic tests, common infections, birth control, menstrual extraction, abortion care, menopause, surgical procedures, home remedies, female ejaculation, the clitoris and universal health problems of women. The full-color photo spread of variations in the cervix

the anatomical jewel

throughout a woman's monthly cycle alone are worth the mere twenty buck investment. *Buy this book.*

Femalia [ISBN 0-940208-15-6], edited by Joani Blank, Down There Press, 938 Howard St. #101, San Francisco, CA 94103. *Femalia* is a collection of full-color cunt photographs. The ages and races of the subjects vary tremendously. "[O]utside of 'men's' magazines [writes Ms. Blank], where the women's genitals were often powdered and half-hidden, and the images often modified and airbrushed, women had no resource for photographic representations of vulvas. . . . Some might wonder how such knowledge benefits women. My many years of doing sex therapy and leading women's sexuality workshops have taught me that without such information a majority of women believe to this day that, in one way or another, their genitals are not quite normal."

The Playbook for Women About Sex [ISBN 0-940208-04-0], by Joani Blank, Down There Press (See address above). "This is a sexual self-awareness book for every woman." Remember those spelling workbooks from the fourth grade? Well, this is very similar, but instead of spelling, you learn about what you want sexually, who you are, what does and does not turn you on. It's very candid, very fun and highly insightful.

Down There Press and Good Vibrations are sisters, both run by the seemingly tireless sexuality valkyrie Joani Blank. They also publish a catalog, *The Sexuality Library,* with over one hundred informative and entertaining sexual self-help and enhancement books. If you order a book from them, the catalog is free, otherwise it's $2.00. You can also get the Good Vibrations store catalog from them.

Herotica: A Collection of Women's Erotic Fiction. Volume I [ISBN 0-940208-11-3] is published by Down There Press (See address above), Volume II [ISBN 0-452-26787-0], Volume III [ISBN 0-452-27180-0] and Volume IV [ISBN 0-452-27181-9] are published by The Penguin Group, Penguin Books U.S.A., Inc., 375 Hudson St., New York, NY 10014. A collection of erotic short stories written by women, for women. Major, major turn-ons in these books. The only drawback to reading any given volume is it takes a long time to finish because you keep having to put it down to masturbate.

Cunt Coloring Book [ISBN 0-86719-371-9], by Tee Corinne, Last Gasp, 2180 Bryant St., San Francisco, CA 94110. This Christmas, buy a *Cunt Coloring Book* for every woman on your list. This book is so fucken cool. It was first published in 1975, so there's no excuse for it not being handed out in human sexuality classes in high school. Says the insanely talented Ms. Corinne, "I first published [these] drawings in a coloring book because a major way we learn to understand the world, as children, is by coloring."

Exhibitionism for the Shy: Show-off, Dress Up and Talk Hot [ISBN 0-940208-16-4], by Carol Queen, Down There Press (See address above). A totally awesome, informative and inspiring book. From the back cover: "[D]emonstrates how to turn sexual modesty to your erotic advantage, whether you're single, partnered or in-between. To discover a new world of erotic

the anatomical jewel

127

experience, you don't have to shed your inhibitions, just exploit them creatively." This is yet another cultural gift from the multifaceted goddess we all fell in love with in the "Whores" chapter.

The New Our Right to Love: A Lesbian Resource Book [ISBN 0-684-80682-7], edited by Ginny Vida, Touchstone Publishing, Rockefeller Center, 1230 Avenue of the Americas, New York, NY 10020. I can't bee-leeve this book is only fourteen dollars. It is so packed with information! "The Spectrum of the Lesbian Experience" includes essays from Lakota, Latina, Jewish, Black, Asian Pacific, young, mid-life, old lesbians, incarcerated lesbians and lesbians with disabilities. There is a fully precious directory of national lesbian organizations, a stunning bibliography, and the chapters cover topics ranging from relationship problems specific to lesbian couples, to lesbians and the law. I *highly* recommend this extremely sensitive, forthright book.

Sex for One: The Joy of Selfloving [ISBN 0-517-88607-3], by Betty Dodson, Crown Publishing Group, Inc., 201 East 50th Street, New York, NY 10022. From the back cover: "Confronting one of our last and most deeply rooted taboos—masturbation—noted sex expert and pro-sex feminist Betty Dodson, Ph.D., takes the shame out of selflove by creating a straightforward and appealing guidebook that reveals masturbation as a satisfying, vital form of sexual expression." Chapters cover topics including masturbation stories, sexual fantasies, masturbation as meditation, orgasms beyond reckoning and making love alone. You simply cannot resist a book with a dedication that reads,

"This book is dedicated to me. Without my selflove, it could not have been written."

Sacred Pleasure: Sex, Myth and the Politics of the Body—New Paths to Power and Love [ISBN 0-06-250283-2], by Riane T. Eisler, HarperCollins Publishers, 10 East 53rd Street, New York, NY 10022. This book is about sex and culture and it's by one of the biggest geniuses of the 20th Century, Riane Eisler! Here's Gloria Steinem's eloquent blurb: "*Sacred Pleasure* makes the links between sacralizing pain and justifying war, between child abuse and sado-masochism, between patriarchy and the war of the sexes, between the intimate and the political. Only by sacralizing pleasure can new links be forged to peace, equality and sexuality." Fucken ayy. There's only one woman on earth who could *possibly* articulate all of this, without losing sight of the sexuality of the *individual* woman, and that woman is the woman who wrote this book: Riane Eisler.

(I included ISBN numbers because they make it easy to order a title from your local independent bookstore, if for some reason you don't want any of these books delivered to your house.)

Videos

How to Female Ejaculate, Blush Entertainment, 526 Castro St., San Francisco, CA 94114, (415) 861-4723. Distributed by Multi-Focus, Inc., 1525 Franklin St., San Francisco, CA 94109, (415) 673 -5100. Also, call Fatale Video at (800) 845-4617 for a free catalog featuring their erotic, woman-made videos. This video taught me how to spew my cuntjuices, and it'll teach you too.

the anatomical jewel

Selfloving: Video Portrait of a Women's Sexuality Seminar, with Betty Dodson, Ph.D., Betty Dodson, Box 1933, Murray Hill, New York, NY 10156. Distributed by Multi-Focus, Inc. In case you haven't gathered, Betty Dodson is the Auto-Eroticism Queen of the Universe.

The Art of Extended Orgasm for Men and Women, by Kathryn Roberts, M.A., NSS Seminars Inc., P. O. Box 620628, Woodside, CA 94062, (415) 851-4751.

Femme Distribution, Inc., c/o Adam and Eve, P. O. Box 800, Dept. Femme, Carrboro, NC 27510, (800) 456-LOVE. Erotic videos for couples, but (here's the crucial part) from a woman's perspective. Free catalog, with a self-addressed stamped envelope.

All right! Hop in the car, get on the horn and make all them cuntdreams of yours come to 3-D, pulsating, glorious, sweaty life.

The generally recognized sexual revolution in the '60s was mostly about men justifying their desire to fuck as many women as humanly possible. A common term arising from this era, after all, was not "husband swapping." The sexual revolution that's long overdue is about women loving themselves alone, with another, whenever, however, forever.

Or at least:

Until death do you part.

Acrimony of Cunts

My mind is very logical. Thoughts are a kind of math to me.
Well before undertaking the task of writing this book,
I understood that certain very specific elements
must be present in order to make a whole.

The element of Whoredom tripped me up a
little. Rape—an element you will be coming upon
shortly—rather hurt. Never did I remotely enter-
tain the notion of omitting either of these elements.

I make this little introduction because I *positively adore* and
consistently seduce the idea of leaving this chapter—concerning
the element of Acrimony—out, out, out. Chills of *ecstasy*
shimmy down my spine when I think about putting a big, fat,
red X over this chapter.

However, my mind is sometimes just this *very weary* high-
school algebra teacher and will not withstand such tomfoolery.

It was very difficult for my sister and I to acknowledge the
insidious nature of acrimony that was (and still can be) present
in our relationship. Jealousy, cattiness and general shitass vibes
were some of the crap-ola emotions we learned to harbor during
our socialization in a culture founded upon destruction. It

required *months* of conversation focused on total honesty, acceptance and love to even approach overcoming negative patterns we grew up with in our personal relationship.

The idea of acknowledging the presence of acrimony between *all women* is pretty dang-awful daunting to me. It extends far past jealousy, cattiness and general shitass vibes into highly oppressive forms of ageism, classism, homophobia, objectification and racism.

I held my sister in my arms on her ride home from being born at the hospital. My sister and me go way back. You, on the other hand, only met me a few short chapters ago. But in comparison to *my* position, *you're* sittin' tight. I have absolutely no idea who you might be, and I'm about to start talking shit to you about nasty things you may perpetuate.

Big sigh.

Still, I know for a fact that being honest and forgiving about acrimony in my personal relationships has freed me and continues to improve the quality of my life intensely. I am privy to the ways acrimony is manifested between women in our culture, and inevitably conclude this sense of freedom and life-improvement holds true on the much broader cultural level as well.

In an interview, Fiona Apple described a shitty period of her life—which she knows she had to experience in order to survive on her terms—as her "dog years."

In the exact same spirit, I present *Cunt*'s dog chapter.

One time I had an Iranian dance teacher named Jaleh. After
class, we'd often have lengthy discussions about culture. As a
result of these conversations, I developed a new perspective on
the standard by which freedom is defined in my country.

I used to think women in fundamentalist Islamic countries,
or societies where genital mutilation is practiced, have it *way
worse* than us ladies in the West. American women can *generally*
wear what we want, fuck who we want, love how we want and
work where we want.

You know, experience "freedom."

Coupled with her religious and political beliefs, that nagging
inspiration known as survival forced Jaleh to flee Iran. There were
many things about her country she detested with all her might and
mien. Malevolence towards women is one thing that ain't veiled in
Iran. Iranian women are shamed, silenced or killed for many
vagrancies Americans guilelessly take for granted. Iranian women
are very consciously aware of gender-explicit oppression.

Therefore:

with so much more at stake, Iranian women have each other's back:
on the street,

in stores,

at celebrations,

everywhere.

When Jaleh first got here, she *completely freaked* about the
meanspiritedness American women project onto one another in
our day-to-day lives. She eventually learned to live with a dull
thud of longing for the *general*, loving, woman vibe that was
once part of her normal reality. Loss of this closeness truly tore
her heart asunder, and Jaleh wondered about the sacrifices

American women make at the behest of our "freedom." What I learned from Jaleh distressed me greatly because I couldn't *imagine* something so precious as an everyday closeness with women, founded in the common knowledge that we all want to survive and thrive in a patriarchal society.

In my country, women don't seem to like each other much at all.

Sucky, sucky, sucky vibes.

I was offered another profound perspective on the actual reality of American women when I interviewed Soraya Miré, a Somali woman who made *Fire Eyes,* a deeply moving, powerful film about genital mutilation.

In countries like mine, the law is *blatantly* against women. What we do have, though, is love and *community.* You never think only of yourself, you always think of your neighbors and family, too.

The problem with a lot of Western women is they think they can *help* me, that they *know what's best* for me. Especially feminist women. They come into conversations waving the American flag, forever projecting the idea they are more intelligent than I am. I've learned that American women look at women like me to hide from their own pain. They can't face their pain, and mine is so obvious, they think they can help me without looking at themselves. But many women in this country are empty. They desperately try to find something to fill the empty space inside them—the loneliness deep inside. In my country, this kind of loneliness does not exist.

In America, women pay *the money that is theirs and no one else's* to go to a doctor who cuts them up so they can create or sustain an image men want. Men are the mirror. Western women cut themselves up voluntarily. In my country, a child is woken up at three in the morning, held down and cut with a razor blade. She has no choice. Western women *pay* to get their bodies mutilated.

When you base your whole self-image on a man—on another human being—how can you expect that person—whether it's a man or a woman—to respect you? How can *you* respect yourself when you do not *have* love and respect for yourself?

One of America's finest cultural phenomena is something called *The Jerry Springer Show*. This is an arena akin to the Roman ones where prisoners fought to the death. On *The Jerry Springer Show*, the audience watches people on a stage as they emotionally and physically maul one another. The viewers at home watch both the audience and the people being mauled. It is the pinnacle of voyeurism, where love, American style, is dissected and pinned down in its most caustic glory.

The Jerry Springer Show is one of my all-time favorite contemporary American anthropological studies.

The show titles change from episode to episode:

"I Want My Man to Stop Going to Strip Clubs."

"I'm Pregnant with His Child and Want Him to Leave His Wife and Three Girlfriends Because I'm More of a Woman Than They Are."

"Gee Honey, Your Mom, Sisters and Best Friends Sure Are

Awesome Good Fucks."

The title never matters because it invariably leads to women physically and verbally attacking each other over some ugly-assed schmuck who's main talent in life is pitting women against each other to bolster his sense of manliness and self-worth.

The Jerry Springer Show is a highly charged and concentrated reflection of a much broader, and generally subtler consciousness under which *all* American women—regardless of sexual orientation—exist.

It's easy enough for the viewers and audience members to look at the woman on the stage and really, really wonder if she's ever even *heard* the term "self-esteem." It's even easier for lesbians to pass judgement on the hapless straight ladies who expend so much energy on something of such dubious merit as a man's unsullied attention, but I've yet to encounter a tribe within *any* community that is not similarly rife with cruelty, possessiveness, jealousy, betrayal, power trips and general shitass vibes.

Some say this is inherent to love, but I say it's inherent to socialization in a destructive cultural setting of ageism, classism, homophobia, objectification and racism.

As Soraya Miré points out, American women indeed learn to look at our pain in others, rather than deal with it as a reality in our lives.

America is a collection of many tribes unified under every conceivable banner—from blood and geography to the Selena fanclub and Harley Davidson motorcycles. Within these tribes, women *may* find inner sanctums of cuntlovin' support.

What interests me, though, is the *standard* of how we

perceive community, and the ways we judge women based on very negative thought patterns we've adopted in order to survive in this society's environment of out-and-out destructive tendencies. As it stands, American women have no frame of reference for relying on each other—cultivating trust, love, standards of beauty and sexuality, economic power and sisterhood.

The fucked-up elements of destruction we learn to view as acceptable are all founded in the exact same basic consciousness or, rather, lack thereof. Ignorance is the most valued consciousness in America. It rends deep chasms of total distrust and perpetuates meanspiritedness bar none. Education, therefore, is the panacea for undermining all manifestations of acrimony in our society.

Every way we see, hear, feel, taste and smell is a *self-reflection*. Our perception awake and asleep is what we, we, we *choose* to perceive. The way we react to any stimulus is the way we *choose* to react.

For a long time, I had a problem with women I perceived as privileged. Rather than harbor and nurture this negative feeling—which would, ultimately, only constitute a bummer in my personal life—I got into reading biographies. I read books about Imelda Marcos, LaToya Jackson, Princess Diana, the Kennedy women and Marjorie Merriweather Post.

It's not like I'm this massive Imelda Marcos fan now, but I have solid ideas about what her life was like when she ruled the Philippines. (And if you think ol' Ferdinand ruled, you be wrong.) Imelda Marcos is no longer just some greedy, capitalist shoe fetishist to me. She is a woman who developed her own set of survival skills, which I clearly do not identify with. Learning something of her childhood and life, however, has made it very difficult for me to pass judgement.

I never imagined Imelda Marcos would communicate any information I would consider valid in my own life, but she taught me a whole new way of looking at women. Imelda wore makeup twenty-four hours a day, seven days a week, with four complete changes, every six hours. She inspired me to appreciate the intricate cultural art form of presentation. The lengths to which she went to be considered beautiful are astonishing. I have complete respect for dedication, precision and commitment, regardless of the fact that Imelda's particular brand represents an insidious form of cunthatred.

Women choose to be catty, cruel, prejudiced, competitive or jealous of each other partly because we grow up learning that negative behavior towards women is perfectly acceptable, and partly because it is a difficult *task* to see ourselves in our perceptions. Seeing ourselves requires effort and commitment.

This unwillingness to see ourselves is greatly exacerbated by the fact that we, quite often, do not see even a remote semblance of ourselves in the images of women commonly found in our society. The women presented to us in ads, TV shows, movies and music videos are powdered and coiffed under standards set by male associations of what is and isn't beautiful.

As a result, many women are scornful and lay blame on women who work in any of these false-image-creating industries. But women who base identity and economic security on a specific standard of "beauty" exist in an industry that is rife with cuntfear. Women choose to work under self-esteem-corroding conditions such as these because cuntfear is highly valued in our society and corporations are willing to pay women exorbitant sums of money for glorifying illusions of beauty men can deal with.

One of my dearest friends used to be one of them fancy übermodels. This experience psychologically damaged her to the degree that I know she would be terribly hurt if I stated her name. I spent a weekend with her a few years ago and she dug out her modeling portfolio for me to look at. The photographs showed this totally posh babe being either sporty, babyish, scary or spicy. I would never, ever, ever, *never* have recognized my dear friend as the woman presented in her portfolio. "They made me," she said, "That was my 'talent': allowing the people who run companies to make me look the way they wanted me to look." When my friend told photographers at shoots that she was interested in photography, they laughed at her. After she quit modeling—and used all that money she saved up as a tidy little nest egg—she became a successful, award-winning art director, designer and photographer.

It doesn't get anybody anywhere to diss models, actresses, dancers and women in general who identify with this male-made standard of beauty. If real images of powerful women being cuntlovin' and beautiful are what women want, the advertising, television, motion picture and music industries must first be infiltrated and revolutionized from the inside out.

It is less *directly* painful to *ourselves* to respond negatively to women than to honestly figure out what other women represents inside of us that we either dislike, fear, wish we "possessed," or are afraid to love.

Another one of my friends used to be almost pathologically uncool about large women. She was rail thin and readily admitted her own fear of being "fat" was the problem. Once she told me, "I think, in a way, I'm jealous because fat women *potentially* love themselves no matter what society says, and I, obviously, do not."

After this conversation, I bought her a bunch of postcard reproductions of paintings depicting large, voluptuous women in erotic poses. She put some of them up in her bathroom. As time passed, her attitude about women and body image started evolving, and she also gained weight. These positive images of women *aided* her in developing a new, healthier perspective, but it was her own courage to be honest with herself that really spurred along positive change in her life.

It is nice to get in the habit of consciously stopping yourself from wishing ill-tidings to a woman, and ask, "What of myself do I see here?" When you can honestly respond to that question without perpetuating self-judgement or nastiness, you is a cuntlover on high.

Adding to the acrimonious nature of growing up in a society that breeds destructive behavior is the fact that the United States is home to more ethnicities than can be found in any other single country on the entire planet. Most nations have the relative luxury of having a population of a few distinct races. I have a friend who is Chinese and Greek, with smatterings of Swiss, Chicana and East Indian blood. She grew up speaking Mandarin and English. I know Korean-Jews and African-American Irish folk. America's ethnicity is the whole kit 'n caboodle, all mixed up in every imaginable combo.

Our national cultural heritage is gloriously schizophrenic.
The result of living as women in an acrimonious,

multiethnic nation is a subconscious negative preoccupation
when dealing with each other. It thus quite naturally escapes us
that while we are so preoccupied, we forsake our collective
power of sheer mass.

This is a bummer for a number of reasons.

American women cannot so much as stand on the same
escalator without the presence of discord—much less design
and implement cuntlovin' economic and legal systems, run
huge cuntlovin' corporations and make sure all of our children
are loved, protected, fed, clothed, educated and tucked into bed
with a sleepytime story that has a happy, cuntlovin' ending.

A significant portion of the acrimony we honor is rooted in
economics.

White people took away the home of Native people who
lived on this land since 𝕿𝖍𝖊 𝕭𝖊𝖌𝖎𝖓𝖓𝖎𝖓𝖌. White people said,
"Sorry, it's this thing called economics, and your home since
𝕿𝖍𝖊 𝕭𝖊𝖌𝖎𝖓𝖓𝖎𝖓𝖌 is now on our property."

White people stole African people from one place and took
them to another, far, far away. White people said, "Sorry, it's
this thing called economics and you are not a human being
anymore, you are our property."

White people snagged Mexico and named it things like
"Southern California," "New Mexico" and "Texas." White people
said, "Sorry, it's this thing called economics, and we'll grudgingly
let you live here but you hafta remember: It's our property."

White people corralled all the Japanese people who were
born in this country same as anybody else. White people said,
"Sorry, it's this thing called economics and what was your

property yesterday is our property today."

So I figure right off the bat: A lot of women in America were raised by mothers who have good, solid-assed reasons for entertaining acrimonious vibrations towards *Las Blancas.*

Good.

Solid-assed.

Reasons.

There is a saying.

It goes, "If you don't face the past, you hafta keep living it."

White women are not readily compelled—much less forced—to face the past. In a white-dominated society, women of color are not generally accorded this option. At some point in life, all children realize skin color plays a major role in one's destiny of survival in this society. Little white girls learn that skin color is a non-issue when one is white. Little girls of color, however, must, at some point, grapple with *why* skin color affects destiny so dramatically. This often leads to facing the past.

I do not think it is culturally healthy or cuntlovin' that facing the past is not *everyone's* responsibility.

One day my friend Harper handed me a piece of paper. She said, "I wrote this at work this morning," as if it might perhaps be a things-to-do list. But it wasn't a things-to-do list at all, and I asked her if I could put it in my book.

It is a fascinating Sunday, or at least seems like it should be. I have been reading *Essence* magazine (the first time in a few years) and something in it inspired me to think of new projects to work on. One is the idea of where you come from, and if you can really go far without establishing in truth—or just in any manner—that sense of belonging somewhere. Like when that man from India was so insistent about asking where I am from, and I ended up at slavery, and I think it was the first time I *really felt* slavery. I mean, I recognized that some of my ancestors had been slaves, but until that day I hadn't felt connected to it past the color of my skin and feeling disgust at the mistreatment and the scope of the cruelty that humans have inflicted on each other—and also embittered in that slaves weren't even allowed the consideration to be recognized as human beings by the colonizers or slavery owners. It was like remembering the tiny pieces of scenes, sound bites and music from the mini-series *Roots* that I viewed before my bedtime as a child . . . a sort of far away horror story. In history lessons this story became worse, with descriptions of the tools used for torture, the neckbrace with bells to keep track of slaves who'd tried to escape, the length of the ships, the number of those herded into the holds, the vomit, the smell, the disease, the death and the wounds—and sometimes mentioned, the note of survival, that continual note of survival that is allowing me to write these words. And more than that note of survival—also my denial and my ability to avoid the remembering because of the pre-recognition of how it makes me sick about humanity in general.

I know I do this about many atrocities.

It wasn't until that day, on my way to Seattle, at a gas station with the two East Indian men I barely knew, as my friend pumped gas, that one of the men asked me where I was from, and I said, "Iowa and D.C." And he said, "No, where are you FROM?" And I said, "Iowa and D.C." And he said, "No, where are you FROM?" And I said , "Iowa and D.C." I explained how I was born in Iowa but had grown up mostly in D.C. "No, ORIGINALLY," he said. Finally understanding that he perhaps made no assumptions that I was a descendant of black slaves, I started to explain there was this thing called slavery in this country and . . . But he was very insistent and interrupted me. "Yes, but YES, WHERE ARE YOU FROM, *your people?*" And I said, "Africa and Germany, but *I don't know*, exactly." As my friend—a white friend—returned to the car, the conversation ended. An uncomfortable silence surrounded me as the conversation turned to the tourist sites in Seattle. I felt lost. I realized this man I had spoken to very likely *knew* what his family was doing in the 1400s. He knew where he was from and where he was grounded, all those miles away from his home. I had just always accepted that I was black in America, and to me, that meant being of questionable mixed heritage, as diverse as the skin tones that defined blackness to me. But this acceptance had never brought me to that question of where I am FROM. And to come to that question in a car at a gas station somewhere between Olympia and Seattle on some random gray day left me silent and lost and feeling the reality of postcolonialism and the reality of the slave trade for the first time in my life.

It is a source of great sadness that my friend is forced to identify with such an ugly treatment of her people in history. If you ever

get into reading history, though, you see how pretty much all
cultures on the planet have pasts filled with bloodshed, rape, war,
enslavement, torture and other symptoms of a destructive
patriarchy encroaching on and dominating everybody else.

There is much sadness in this world.

If you have the courage to ask, Rigoberta Menchú, Sojourner Truth, Wilma Mankiller, Jacqueline Woodson, Mary
Crow Dog and Kathy Acker will tell you:

There is much sadness in this world.

During the '60s and '70s Steve Biko was one of the leaders in
South Africa's Black Consciousness movement. In the biography
Biko, by Donald Woods, I found that Black Consciousness and
cuntlove share many of the same basic principles. Woods writes,
"Many would prefer to be color-blind; to them skin pigmenta-
tion is merely an accident of creation. To us, it is something
much more fundamental. It is a synonym for subjection, an
identification for the disinherited." (Woods, 1979, 37)

I can relate to this because the presence of estrogen in my
body is a synonym for subjection and identification for the
disinherited.

However, America was colonized by male and white people.
All women experience alienation due to the overwhelming *male*
standard based in this history. Women of color experience alienation for the overwhelming *white* standard, too. I consider it
perfectly acceptable to expect men of all ethnicities and classes to
educate themselves and take responsibility for their individual role
in women's oppression. I likewise consider it perfectly acceptable
to expect white women of all classes to take responsibility for our

individual role in the oppression of women of color. Women of color *have no call* to trust white women until white women take a gander at the world around them, investigate, learn and annihilate ignorance founded in being white in a society where the perspective and voice presented to the general public is white.

Still and too, acrimony between white women and women of color is but one of many pits in our potentially delicious cherry pie. Within each tribe, racial acrimony is present. Acrimony is a way of general socialized American life until you decide you don't want it that way no more. All races of people are divided and isolated from one another.

It is the house that Jack built.

Chinese women might harbor negative stereotypes about Filipina women, who may not think nice things about Jewish women, who might grow up thinking ill of Moslem women, who may think lesbians are the scourge of the earth, who might think women married to Promise Keepers are the incarnation of evil, who may think teenagers who get abortions should be sentenced to hard labor at juvey.

And on and on.

In school we learn that one of the best survival strategies is being part of a clique. With our friends, we create a little, tiny world with codes for conduct, morality, dress, communication, ethnicity and sexuality. We then learn to judge everyone else who is not part of our little world by the standards that are acceptable to us. This is called "divide and conquer," and happens to be exactly how male, white patriarchal society operates. When you choose not to see how you, yourself, perpetuate this social model, your world assuredly becomes—or remains—small, "safe," persnickety, judgemental and uninspiring.

How else could Bill Gates decide it was a good idea to build such a temporal item as a sprawling multimillion-dollar house for his one-child nuclear family, in a society where kids in schools hafta *share* textbooks published in 1987? In his little, tiny world, it is acceptable to squander money and responsibility in this manner. I consider it an embarrassing display of karmic retardation when someone invests so much money in something that could *burn to ashes in a fire,* while human beings continue to starve and go insane on the streets.

We learn to justify many preposterous actions within the small worlds we are encouraged to create throughout life.

> You can't be a solitary human being. [We're] all linked. . . .
> Because of this deep sense of community, the harmony of
> the group is a prime attribute. And so you realize that
> anything that undermines the harmony is to be avoided as
> much as possible. Anger and jealousy and revenge are
> particularly corrosive, so you try . . . to enhance the human-
> ity of the other, because in that process, you enhance your
> own. (*The Progressive,* February 1998, 19)

We are *all* raised under the influences of negative standards set by our culture. We naturally fail to note that all the women around us are dealing with the exact same things, in entirely different ways.

If you want to find out how your oppression infringes on your freedom, walk into the bathroom, stare deeply into your eyes, and face your pain without blame. Don't go feeling sorry

the anatomical jewel

147

for them ladies in Saudi Arabia and Pakistan until you do this first. Don't be dissin' on übermodel-types with silicone titties until you do this first. Don't sneer at women from a class or ethnicity different from your own, at lesbians, bi-women, straight women, fat women, skinny women, old women or young women until you do this first.

There will remain much sadness in the world until people are willing to rise to the task of facing the world's pain in the bathroom mirror.

American culture is very, very, very, very, very beautiful.

I am thankful and happy to live in a society where so many perspectives and bounties of educational resources are available. My society honors the public library system. I have *every* opportunity to learn about things of which I was raised to be ignorant.

Wheee!

In one American afternoon, I might encounter Cibo Matto sounding out from a used bookstore, a Peruvian band attracting a crowd on the street corner, Missy Elliott pulsating from one of those cars that are really state-of-the-art sound systems on wheels, while a queer Lithuanian-Basque Vietnam vet caterwauls Barbra Streisand songs in the doorway of an office building.

Wheee!

I believe it is possible for women who live in this beautiful culture to access a forsaken—but still inherent—love and respect for each other based on the sole criteria of what our cunts have been through for the past few thousand years.

Which segues into a commandment the bible, koran and torah writers plumb done forgot to include . . .

Rape Not Cunts

While writing about orgasms at four o'clock in the morning, I ran out of soymilk for my coffee. I was tired. I needed a bike ride and coffee to keep da pace. At 10 a.m., I would've encountered no internal deliberation. The wee-dawn hours, however, are definitely past curfew time for women on solo ventures.

Still.

I didn't want to drink my coffee black. I didn't want to be afraid of going to the grocery store just because I have a cunt.

So I:

1. Put a beanie on my head to camouflage my female-ness, at least from a distance.
2. Did the ol' once over in the mirror to ascertain that my sweats were baggy enough to hide the contours of my fine, round, womanly ass.
3. Tied my running shoes nice and tight, in case I might have to kick or bolt.
4. Donned a loose, black, butchy-poo jacket.
5. Stuffed the five medium-sized rocks I keep on hand

for excursions such as this into the pockets of said
jacket.

6. Made sure the tires on my bike had enough air in
    them, in the event that I'd have to race to safety.

All six of these steps are part of a survival tactic I have
incorporated into my lifestyle because: *I can't stand the fact that
the danger of having a cunt is threatening enough to keep me from
doing as I please.*

Though I've lived away from home for over a decade, my
mother still has a tizz when I go out by myself after 11 p.m. So
I don't tell her it drives me insane to allow the possibility of
being raped to dictate my will.

I Do the Best I Can.

My friend Esther, who lives in the same apartment
building, gets off work at three in the morning. She rarely goes
to bed before eight. The last step in this particular survival
tactic is calling her.

"Esther, I'm going to the store. If I'm not home safe and
sound in fourteen minutes (we have it timed), come find me.
I'll be riding up Olive and down Broadway."

"Okey-doke. It's 4:18. Go. Oh, wait. Pick me up a pack of
smokes, will ya? Go."

Esther and I have never discussed my motive for calling
and letting her know I'm going to the grocery store. One night,
the need simply arose. How telling it is that *not once* did it occur
to Esther to question me. As women raised in a violent,
patriarchal culture we inherently understand the risks one may
encounter when one has a cunt.

I ride my bike to the grocery store. The cashiers are used to seeing me at unseemly hours. They let me park my bike inside, by the greeting cards. I feel safe in the grocery store, but at the same time, I know not to assume this to be a fact.

I go to great lengths to make it seem like I'm not fettered to the violence—and subsequent injustice of the American legal system—that my cunt can potentially inspire.

But I ain't foolin' nobody.

Certainly not myself.

I'm fully privy to the reality that my cunt's presence on my body can inspire people with cocks to attempt to exert their power by attempting to humiliate me. I have no illusions about what happens to women in "the wrong place at the wrong time." I have seen too many movies, read too many newspapers, watched too many episodes of *Unsolved Mysteries*.

I know too many women who have been raped.

I do not pretend too realistically that I am free to go where I please. At least, not without taking extreme precautionary measures.

Purchasing soymilk for my coffee at four o'clock in the morning, then, is an act of rebellion.

A foolhardy and mundane one, perhaps.

Like I said, I Do the Best I Can.

When I was twenty, my mother told me she had been raped. Five years passed before I mustered the courage to write about it.

It is highly distressing to learn the sacred, holy place where you lived during your first nine months on this planet was ruthlessly pillaged long before you were conceived.

It makes you wonder if there exists a safe place.

She was nine.

She was nine.

My mother was nine.

Over a Christmas holiday, Mom and I were talking in the kitchen. I don't remember that we were discussing anything in particular. Liz popped her head in to say goodbye. She was going to a party, dressed to the nines in a satin slipdress.

Our mother stopped in mid-innocuous-sentence and stared. Liz and I stared back. Mom looked down at her hands. (Momspeak interpretation: **Something Is Up.**)

Big sigh.

"I really wish you wouldn't go out dressed like that."

In the past, my sister and I would have rolled our eyes at each other and made light of it. Mom said things like this pretty much whenever she saw us dressed scantily for a party. This exchange had taken place hundreds of times.

But we could tell from her voice that tears were welling up in her eyes. This wasn't something we could shrug off as Mom's "overprotectiveness." There was suddenly a **Big Problem** in the kitchen.

Liz put her purse on the table and felt for a chair.

Neither of us could tear our eyes from our mother.

"Mom . . . " my sister spluttered.

I whispered, "Mom, what's wrong?"

Both of us were crying, but we had no idea why.

Nobody went to any party that night.

Two men saw her walking home from school in her Catholic girls' school uniform. The temptation was too much for them. The men pulled her into some bushes in Hyde Park and raped her.

Our mother, our, our, our beautiful mother.

Two men did that to her.

She was nine, she was nine.

She had no words to correspond with the defilement. She didn't come across sufficient vocabulary for an entire decade. She walked home, changed her clothes and never breathed a word to anyone until she was in college. In the meantime—that is, throughout her adolescence—my mother relied solely on rape's best pal, silence, to help her survive this experience. She buried her silence deep because what else could she do.

When the Goddess eventually blessed her with two daughters, oh, how she watched us.

She said, "You two always thought I was paranoid, but how could I tell you why I was like that, how could I hurt you when you were so little and free? Then as you got older, I didn't know *when* to tell you. I knew it would make you cry like this."

We sobbed from the pits of our guts.

The whole time we were growing up, she attended seminars and clinics focused on rape to help her deal with the pain she sequestered in a dark region of her heart when she was a child. She had to learn how to control her fear that "something would happen" to my sister or me.

Hawk, mother hawk.

A new panorama slammed into my heart. I remembered years and years of relentless warnings: "Don't take short-cuts," "Come straight home from school," "Never walk past vans," "If a car is following you, cross the street and run to a neighbor's house. If you aren't near a neighbor's house, run into the middle of the street and scream 'FIRE!' at the top of your lungs."

A childhood memory assailed me.

I was eight. One morning, my friend Kit and I went to the mall to buy our moms' gifts for Mother's Day. We ended up dawdling awfully long, and I didn't get home until dinnertime. My mother was standing in front of our house. There was no color in her face. Her eyes were blind terror. She swept me into her arms and hugged all of the breath out of me. Then she slapped me across the face.

It stung.

My father was cruising the neighborhood in a cop car. He came home and immediately grounded me to my room for a week.

My mother didn't utter a word.

That week I brooded in my room.

I thought they were overreacting.

In other words:

Because of the action of two completely unknown males in the year 1948, I was slapped across the face and grounded to my room for a week in 1974.

A different way of looking at this is:

I was raised by a woman who was held down in a park and raped when she was a little girl. While the consequences of this event became, for Liz and me, a Grand Duchess Overtone in our upbringing, the two men who raped our mother have no idea either of us exist on the planet to have been raised under the shadow of their action.

A further perspective might be:

A man could, feasibly, sacrifice his coffee break raping a woman.

That woman would then spend her entire life dealing with it.

So would her daughters.

So would theirs.

This distribution of power is not acceptable.

The Sioux believe a people cannot be vanquished unless the spirit of woman is broken.

Though rape is viewed merely as a crime, it is the fundamental, primal, most destructive way to seize and maintain control in a patriarchal society.

When wars are declared, everyone involved in the declaration assumes women will be raped. Invading soldiers do not necessarily rape women to hurt us, per se. Women are raped to stymie the morale of husbands, fathers and sons. Women's bodies are considered solely in regard to how they affect men. In the context of war, rape literally plants the seed of the invader in the body of a people. The secret weapon of war is spiritually crippling an entire nation of human beings and generations to come by sexually assaulting as many women and girls as possible.

Men use our bodies to bear witness to their power.

America was founded on the bodies of women: African women, Jewish women, Native women, Latina women, Chicana women, Asian women, European women. Grandmother, grandmother, grandmother, grandmother, grandmother, grandmother, grandmother.

Guatemalan, Bosnian, Vietnamese women know war.

Pretty much every nation in this world was established by war.

How many women do you think that is?

In 1993, a woman named Mia Zapata, the lead singer of a rock band called the Gits, was found dead in Seattle, Washington. I lived in Seattle and wrote for a local weekly newspaper at the time.

It sucked very hard.

I clung to the fact that newspaper and word-of-mouth accounts did not mention the word "rape." Strangled, murdered, killed. Those words were already quite unbearable. No sooner would the word "rape" flit through my mind than I'd remind myself none of the newscasters mentioned it.

I felt the world could still seem a halfway decent place, so long as Mia Zapata wasn't raped.

I never knew her, never went and saw her band. Never listened to her music, not even after she died. But Seattle's a small city, and we shared a number of friends. She was generally associated with things like outspokeness, creativity, powerful expression, talent and loving inspiration.

She was strong.

A Whore found
her body
in
an
alley.

I knew no woman who was not profoundly grief-stricken by her death. This was the feeling *before* the word "rape" was associated with Mia Zapata's death.

In the autumn following Mia's death, I interviewed the band 7 Year Bitch in the very tavern where Mia spent her last night. That is when I learned, once and for all, beyond a shadow of a doubt, yes, Mia Zapata was raped.

Even though women are raped and murdered every day, I tried really, really hard to pretend it didn't happen in my world, where I live, to women I see when I'm walking down the street each day.

I don't do that anymore.

In the final analysis, it took far more negative energy to live in denial than to face my fear and acknowledge the astounding prevalence of rape in my culture.

Now, I routinely assume that if the cancer of a man's soul condones the murder of a living, breathing, hoping, loving, fighting, singing, dancing, searching, yearning human being, the chances are pretty slim his cancer has spared his cock.

Now, when I hear of a man murdering a woman, I assume that he raped her unless I read the fucken coroner's report myself.

A definition for "martyr" according to my trusty 1965 Random House Dictionary is: "One who is put to death or endures great suffering on behalf of any belief, principle or cause."

The greatest purposes martyrs serve are teaching, inspiring and giving strength to those who live on after their death.

In contrast to the killing of Dr. King or Malcolm X, there is little to support the idea that Mia Zapata was raped and murdered because of her personal (that is, political) actions as a woman. Nevertheless, her unspeakably tragic death is symbolic in that very mien. Ms. Zapata was a pillar of strength—a living, thriving, raging testimony of the power of unleashed artistic expression.

That she was killed in a horrible way psychologically tortured an entire community of women. Mia Zapata's life and death moshed into a collective consciousness.

Being part of a community that was grieving the brutal murder of one of its priestesses had a massive impact on my life. I could no longer contain my fear and rage. This was sickeningly exacerbated by another incident, which took place a few months later.

A woman parked near her apartment building late at night. As she was getting out of her car, she noticed two men up to some kind of mischief. She judged the distance to safety and thought she could negotiate it.

She was wrong.

The two men grabbed her, put her in her car and drove away. They cruised 'round the city for hours, taking turns raping the woman in the back seat of her car. When they were done, they took her to a high-school field, stabbed her in the head repeatedly with a Phillips screwdriver, and left her for dead.

She did not die.

She had to learn everything all over again. She will prob-ably never function in the way she had once always assumed she would.

One kinda takes it for granted that since one learned to read in first grade, one probably won't ever have to learn to read again.

For many, many women in the Pacific Northwest, it grew increasingly unavoidable to confront the issue of rape in our culture.

Directly after Ms. Zapata's death, the organization Home Alive was founded. Their mission statement reads:

> Home Alive is a collective of performance and visual artists (and other freaks) hell bent on fighting all forms of violence and oppression including rape, domestic abuse, gay/lesbian bashing, racism, etc. We support people choosing any form of self defense that is necessary to survive in any given situation. Examples of self defense are verbal boundary setting, walking friends to cars or houses, locking doors, planning escape routes, de-escalation techniques, using pepper spray, physical striking techniques, fighting, yelling, martial arts, knives, guns, other weapons—ANYTHING that keeps us alive.
>
> Since the brutal rape and murder of Mia Zapata on July 7, 1993, we are dedicated to presenting an on-going series of high intensity music, art, spoken word, theater, film and video events that raise money to provide our community with free and affordable self defense workshops, educational material, resource information and a nagging reminder that none of us are safe.

In Seattle, Olympia and Portland, self-protection classes became *de rigueur*. In Portland, a beautiful compilation album

the anatomical jewel

called *Free to Fight* was released. Home Alive later released a compilation album, *The Art of Self-Defense*, featuring the work of many regional and national artists. Creative expression rolled to a boil, and women performed en masse. Rage crested at the forefront of songs, words, movements.

A lot of brilliant women all thinking about the same thing at the same time is very powerful. This is how change happens. Rather than underscore this to queendom come, I dedicate the next few pages to the voices of some of the women who lived in the area at the time.

Because I didn't know Mia, I didn't feel the intensity of grief a lot of people around here felt, but it made me really paranoid to the point where I felt I was losing my mind. For about three months, I lived in a state of terror, where I became afraid of everyone I knew, everyone I met, everyone I saw. I even became afraid of myself. I felt this vast rage, like I wanted to kill someone, but I didn't know who. That was very frightening. I'd never felt like that before.

But what I did was, I wrote a play called *Again*. It was all about sexual violence and abuse and the fact that your own sexuality seems to invite danger. I spent a lot of time asking myself how I can still be a sexual person, while at the same time warding off dangerous situations. Having my sexuality at the surface is very important to me, and I'm not willing to give it up. Somewhere inside myself, I suddenly believed that in order to get through this life without being raped, I had to give up my sexuality.

So, I wrote *Again*. I didn't pursue having it produced because I wasn't sure that it wouldn't make people feel more afraid and disempowered, which is not what I'm trying to do with my work at all.

Recently, my friend was telling me he was reading this book about serial killers. When he'd read about half of it, he threw the book out the eleventh-story window of his apartment because he felt it was some kind of evil totem. He wasn't learning anything from it, it was only exacerbating a fear he already had, and the book was debilitating him.

The way he described it to me sounded like that terror I felt after Mia's death, but also what I felt like when I was finished writing *Again*. It helped me, the individual, deal with my fear, but as a piece of art, I felt more like it would debilitate society in general.

There wasn't enough hope in it.

I still have so much fear of my sexuality. I hope to someday produce something to honor my sexuality, but right now, my relationship with my sexuality is colored by how other people respond to it, which I distrust greatly.

People seem to have a hard time responding to a woman's sexuality without having the desire to literally touch it. I guess in some ways, sexuality implies that, but I don't think sexuality necessarily invites someone else to participate. I don't want people to interpret my work as an invitation to fuck me.

I did read *Again* a few times, at a couple small theaters and a nightclub. There's one part where the woman character is describing what she finds erotic to a man who wants to have sex with her, but she does not want to have sex with him. She talks about listening to the rain gush into a gutter, watching a woman dip her finger in her latté and lick the foam off her finger, and someone taking their shirt off and having another one on underneath. She's telling him all these things that have nothing to do with intercourse, and often nothing to do with other people, in an effort to explain her idea of sexual eroticism to him.

After I read this at the nightclub, a friend of mine told me an acquaintance of his came up after my performance and said, "Who's that? I'd like to bone her." I was amazed. Was this guy listening to what I was saying? The character was telling a man exactly what she did not want from him and this guy thought I, the writer, would want that? That I'd want to be "boned"?

In *Letters to a Young Poet*, Rilke says, "The highest form of love is to be the protector of another person's solitude." That's what I want. For other people to love each other without having to *partake* in them, to *possess* them, to allow them to be their own inside their solitude, to protect that. I wish people respected each other's aloneness. I wish I could write something very beautiful and erotic without worrying about people wanting to use me to fulfill some fantasy—which I have no control over, and often, has nothing to do with me—inside themselves. (Kristen Kosmas, writer and performer)

When Mia died, it was like, "This is something that happens to *other people.*" I mean, it happens all the time. A woman is raped in this country every four minutes, but for someone you know to be raped and murdered, someone so strong . . . It's hard to talk about the effect Mia's death had on other women in the community. Mia's rape and murder wasn't just one isolated event, unto to itself. It happened in a really vocal, outspoken community of women, who were already trying to find their voice. A lot of people say, "I didn't know her, but I felt moved to do something about her dying the way she did."

There's also a general, unifying feeling of rage in the community. Rape and murder will inspire that, regardless. Like [the young woman mentioned earlier who was abducted by two men]. She's still alive, and there was a huge response to her attack.

I teach self-defense in the community to instill in women the idea that no one has any more or less power than anyone else. What happened to [the young woman mentioned earlier], to Zolah Lippe [a Seattle writer who committed suicide in 1995], Kristin Pfaff [Hole's bass player, who overdosed on heroin] and Stephanie Sargent [7 Year Bitch's guitar player, who also overdosed on heroin]—it's all related in the sense that within the span of every minute, a woman dies in some fucked-up way, based upon her belief that she is powerless.

I started performing because I had to. It was a natural progression of what I was already doing. I make a difference and have an effect—it's not that I think people will see me perform and view violence against women in a completely different way, but I am definitely part of a larger thing which effects change. Often people either don't want to, or aren't used to seeing women angry. Not emotional, not upset, just angry. Not reactionary anger, necessarily, the anger of just being a woman. My anger serves me. It gives me a lot of energy. Sometimes, it hurts, which is the flip side of the same coin. But, I'm happy. I like my life. I like being free to express my rage. (Cristien Storm, spoken word performer, self-protection instructor, co-founder of Home Alive)

My life profoundly changed [after Mia Zapata's death] because Home Alive started out of that, and it's been one of the major focuses of my life.

My personal habits have changed dramatically as well. I used to hop on the bus alone late at night, walk around late at night. I don't do that at all anymore. I always ask my female friends how they're getting home at night and if they don't have a ride, I'll drive them. I never leave my friends without asking them if they need a ride home and they do the same for me. The whole "Okay, see you later, bye!" thing just does not happen in my life anymore.

Self-defense is something you have to work on consistently and practice. Cristien [Storm] is a fine example of a woman who practices self-defense. I never took self-defense before Home Alive started.

I've still never shot a loaded gun, but I've taken gun classes. I respect other people's choices to have a gun in their life and use it as a form of self-defense. I know a lot of women who have guns and that's their business. I don't feel comfortable with guns. However, we live in a society where guns are quite prevalent. You never know when there's gonna be a situation where a gun might be present, so you might want to know how to use one.

A big part of the philosophy of Home Alive is that people have to make their own choices about self-defense. Anything they're comfortable with, that makes them feel safe and keeps them alive is the right choice. (Gretta Harley, musician, co-founder of Home Alive)

A couple of years ago, I woke up at three in the morning to this knock on my door. My friend was standing there, scared and crying. She hadn't been feeling well and couldn't sleep, so she had gone for a walk. She was walking by the park a few blocks from here and this car started stalking her. Later she didn't know why, but she thought she'd be safe if she hid in the women's bathroom. He found her and went into the bathroom. They struggled for a while and I think she did the "I could be your sister" thing and he finally went away. That's when she came to my house. I imagine her walking those three short blocks and how frightened she must have been. Later on, we had to go back to the bathroom to find her glasses, which she lost when she was struggling with the man. That was very terrifying, even though there were three of us.

The next night was the Olympia Art Walk and the streets were full of people walking around town. I'd been projecting images on the Arts Center's wall across the street from my apartment building, so we worked feverishly all that afternoon making a slide show to let people know what had happened the night before. We projected a description of the man and his car, when and where he tried to attack my friend. It was really strange to see people's reactions to it because since we didn't have much time, the images were really cartoony so people kinda laughed until they understood we made this because our friend almost got raped the night before, three blocks away from where they were standing. Then they were like, "Oh, that's right over there."

No matter how strong you are, no matter how safe you are, no matter how lucky or crafty you are, you still might be put in a position where you could get hurt. That kinda might be depressing to some people, but I think as long as you're aware of that reality, you might actually make it to the moon if you're a rocket scientist. [Laughs.] You might survive.

Also, realizing that you might not have everything you need to survive makes it more likely that you'll seek out other people to help you. Like when my friend came to my door that night. She could've run up to the park and screamed, knowing someone would've opened their window and helped her, but she knew we'd hold her instead of just providing her with a place to be removed from the danger.

I thought about that a lot when I was working on the *Free to Fight* album, which is this really great collaboration project Candyass Records put together. It was so cool when I got this lovely letter from Donna Dresch, saying they were gonna be putting out this record and asking me to contribute. I was like, "Oh, wow!" I don't really know how the whole thing came about, but it seemed like a great idea to me, an amazing thing to be a part of.

Anyway, during the *Free to Fight* tour, there were self-defense workshops before each show. Self-defense is something I've never taken the time out to learn, but this was really cool because it was right there. It was very beautiful. Everybody lined up in three rows, the whole room was shouting in unison. Three girls would go up at the same time and do the move while everyone else yelled and cheered them on. So many voices. It made me so happy. The workshops made people feel good about themselves, like, "I can do this!" It wasn't like, "You better do this because the world's scary and people are out to get you." It wasn't inspired by paranoia or anything. It taught me that I already do a lot of these things, I just never thought of it as self-defense before. Everybody has their own way of defending themselves, they just never think of it as such. Simple things like walking tall, talking loudly, crossing the street.

Last night I was at a show in Seattle. I went outside to get some fresh air and there was a girl standing there near me. These two guys walked up and asked her what was going on inside and all these other questions. They weren't being assholes or anything, but I stayed near, even though I'd gotten enough fresh air. I didn't want to leave her alone outside with these two guys. I stood there until they left and then I went back inside. That was self-defense. (Nikki McClure, performance artist)

If the violent rape and murder of one woman has an
impact on the lives of thousands of her sisters, then at the very,
very least, she did not die in vain. Unfortunately, for every
solitary woman whose death inspires something other than
cavernous silence, millions of women are raped, maimed,
mutilated and murdered without garnering so much as a
paragraph in the local newspaper.

There is no Howardina Stern on the airwaves every morning
instigating passionate, pro-active, cuntlovin' dialogues about
rape in our culture. News helicopters hover over the scenes of
bank robberies and traffic accidents, not parks where a woman
was raped. Cities bestow awards of valor to fire fighters and good
samaritans, not women who elude, maul or successfully
prosecute would-be rapists.

On the back cover of Migael Scherer's courageous and
brilliant book, *Still Loved by the Sun: A Rape Survivor's Journal*,
Ursula K. Le Guin says, "The power of the harasser, the abuser,
the rapist depends above all on the silence of women."

Contemplate the simplicity, depth and truth of this statement:
The power
depends
on the silence.
Silence is our focal point of attack.
Silence is the unlocked door through which intruders enter
and pillage the sacred temple of womankind.

The threat of rape lurked around my childhood in relentless
warnings and admonishments. When my mother told me she had

been raped, I understood the source of the fear I grew up with.

Like many women, it saddened me to feel "lucky" that rape remained a threat, but not an actual occurrence, in my personal life. I was further saddened by the fact that the very reason, I believe, neither my sister nor I has been raped is in part due to our mother's experience. She actively, consciously, ferociously protected us. Long before we knew our mother had been raped, Liz and I developed a sixth sense for dangerous situations. I am thankful for that. I believe it has aided me on a number of occasions. I wish, however, it was not initially inspired by fear and feelings of powerlessness.

Fear and powerlessess.

Silence.

Rape.

Cunthatred.

It's time for this to end.

When I started this chapter, I was re-studying Pippi Longstocking. Partly because of my childhood, I would like to formally invoke Ms. Longstocking's attitude to serve as the Grand Duchess Overtone for the duration of this book:

"Have you ever seen hair like hers? Red as fire! And such shoes," Bengt continued. "Can I borrow one? I'd like to go out rowing and I haven't any boat." He took hold of one of Pippi's braids but dropped it instantly and cried, "Ouch, I burned myself."

Then all five boys joined hands around Pippi, jumping up and down and screaming, "Redhead! Redhead!"

Pippi stood in the middle of the ring and smiled in the friendliest way. Bengt had hoped she would get mad and begin to cry. At least she ought to have looked scared. When nothing happened he gave her a push.

"I don't think you have a very nice way with ladies," said Pippi. And she lifted him in her strong arms—high in the air—and carried him to a birch tree and hung him over a branch. Then she took the next boy and hung him over another branch. The next one she set on a gatepost outside a cottage, and the next she threw right over the fence so that he landed in a flower bed. The last of the fighters she put in a tiny toy cart that stood by the side of the road. . . . The boys were absolutely speechless with fright.
(Lindgren, 1950, 32-33)

There are two things women can do to facilitate the end of rape as an inevitable—even acceptable—aspect of our culture. The first is relatively easy, but the second will take a bit of serious cuntlove to come to fruition.

One out of eight movies produced in Hollywood contains a rape scene. In American cinema, rape scenes tend to be violently eroticized, and often have nothing to do with the main plot of the film. When viewing a rape scene, scads of men feel confused and disgusted with themselves if it turns them on.

Eugene Chadbourne, a columnist for *MAXIMUMROCKNROLL* eloquently discussed a male perspective on Hollywood rape scenes. In response to *The Accused*, he stated:

After more than an hour of the film, the audience is shown the rape. There she was, Jodie Foster, stretched out on top of a pinball machine with a bunch of assholes holding her down. The first few shots of her breasts and the man kissing her and slurping around were undeniably erotic. . . . I kept wondering why I was turned on. I explained it to myself that I just knew it wasn't a real rape, [but] . . . if the whole center of the film, a supposedly brutal and disgusting rape, turns on even one person in the audience just a little bit, then the film has completely missed its mark.

A few weeks later, I saw an Australian film entitled *Shame*. This was also about rape . . . the differences between these two films were many, but one basic thing was that the makers of *Shame* chose not to show the rape, the makers of *The Accused* made it their climactic scene. *(MAXIMUMROCKNROLL,* March 1990)

Another non-Hollywood film that deals with rape in a responsible way is *The Bandit Queen*, which is based on a true story. The protagonist, Phoolan Devi, was raped for a number of days by high-caste men in an Indian village. The camera focused on the door of the room she was kept in, with images of man after man entering and exiting. The point of her assault was clearly, horrifically made, and there was absolutely nothing erotic about it. (Her gang was allegedly responsible for later assassinating all of these men.)

In general, with the exception of a few films—*Thelma and Louise* comes to mind—rape scenes found in American cinema are filmed from the p.o.v. of men, who evidently experience some kind of personal gain by humiliating women. I do not know if the men who make movies enjoy humiliating individual actresses, or if it is a symbolic show of power over women in general. I do know that too many movies contain scenes that deal with rape in an unrealistic, male-fantasy-based manner.

Women viewers subjected to such scenes may experience any emotion between utter indifference and profound grief. It is safe to assume, however, that underneath any emotional response is a basic assumption of powerlessness. We are powerless to help the woman on the screen, unable to change her destiny, we cannot kill the piece of shit who violates her. We are forced to watch the pillage of one of our sisters unfold, under the charmed auspices of something executives in Hollywood refer to as a plot.

Perhaps also, we are unwilling to take responsibility for something we are brought up to think of as inevitable.

The last rape scene I ever saw was in *Last Exit to Brooklyn*. The gang-rape of Jennifer Jason Leigh's character physically sickened me. When someone tells me about a great new movie, I almost always asks if there's a rape scene in it. Once this information is obtained, I can gauge whether or not this might, indeed, be a great new movie. Boycotting movies with rape scenes has enriched the quality of my life.

I don't need to see that shit.

And so, I don't.

We do not need to see our sisters up there on the screen being overpowered and assaulted by bad, scary men. We do not need to see good, righteous men saving our sisters in the knick of time, or achieving "justice" for us in the courtroom.

It does not serve us.

There are a couple of options here.

Option #1:

If you know a movie will contain a rape scene, forego seeing it altogether. If you unwittingly go to a movie that contains a rape scene, leave the theater and demand your money back from the manager. Let the manager know you will not pay to see women raped. Write a letter to the president of the movie theater's distribution company. Feel free to incite your friends. Especially if you're a teenager and you organize a huge protest. The ten o'clock news likes nothing more than high-school girls causing a ruckus in the name of social change. Even though it may seem like a faraway, remote place, Hollywood is a very small town with very big ears.

Movies featuring women who are strong, ass-kicking controllers of destiny are not so hard to come by these days, so it's not like such a boycott would encumber our movie-going habits. There are plenty of wonderful films to choose from. It's far healthier to watch *The Long Kiss Goodnight* five times than to bother yourself with *Showgirls* or *Kids* once. *La Femme Nikita* and *Gloria* are excellent classics. *Set it Off, Freeway, Girls Town* and *Bound* are part of a very welcome influx of excellent, cuntlovin' movies produced in the 1990s.

Option #2:

Plan to attend movies that you know contain rape scenes. Go with a bunch of your friends. Once the rape scene is underway,

the anatomical jewel

stand up and scream. Freak. Loudly narrate your own version of what is happening on the screen:

"Now she is pounding his face into the metal stairs of the fire escape. Her shoe is off. Ooo! Spiked heel to the temple!!! Look at all that blood oozing from his head!" Etc. . . .

When the scene is over, march to the manager. Demand your money back based on the affront to women you were forced to witness. Continue making a huge, articulate scene in the lobby. When all your friends get their refunds, leave quietly, but continue to be cranky about it.

If our buying dollars are not squandered on that which does not serve us, sooner or later, the gentlemen in Hollywood may see the light. However, in the not too unrealistic event that gentlemen in Hollywood never see the light, our money can be used to generate more movies that serve us. There is an *entire regiment* of women in the motion picture industry struggling very hard to deliver such products to us. Let us, shall we, constructively focus on this branch of American cinema. At the same time, we also can choose to offer constructive and loud criticism to the present movie machine that makes billions of dollars off us each year.

You may have already figured this out, but the whole reason I ever felt inspired to sit down and write this book originated with the rape of my mother. I couldn't think of any other way to exact vengeance on the men who hurt her, my sister and me so deeply.

I have thought long and hard about why women are objects of violence.

I've been through the Blaming Men phase and then I passed on to the Blaming Women Phase. Neither phase did me, as an individual, much good. So then, I guess for sheer lack of imagination, I blamed myself. That didn't last long though, 'cause one night I was falling asleep and this cherry '68 Impala Lowrider cruised around in my head, and it had a bumper sticker that said:

𝔅lame is lame with a "b"

So I thought to explore an option I hadn't considered before. I decided to love myself. To love my cunt. To love everything it does and represents.

That seemed to do a lot of good, and led me to ask myself: What is the result of women loving our cunts, en masse?

There is no place for rape in a society filled with women who love our cunts. Women can be kicked when we are down, but no one is stupid or strong enough to kick us when we are standing up, all, together.

This may sound idealistic in some regards, but cuntlove envisions no mass utopia. Cuntlove is about the individual and her community. Cuntlove is about the power of you, your sisters, cousins, daughters and intimate friends. Cuntlove is not distant rhetoric found in books and debate halls. Cuntlove is in your head, on your heart, between your legs.

Aldous Huxley, a white male writer with the ensuing sense of entitlement for which white males are famous, said, "Liberties are not given, they're taken."

In the past, women have relied on individual men and patriarchal judicial systems to fight rape.

Unfortunately, this nets exactly the same result as when I got my brothers and sister to lean towards the Baskin Robbins as our family car approached that big, gorgeous pink-'n-white "31 Flavors" sign.

At the time, I thought the sudden redistribution of our body weight would affect the momentum of our Volkswagen van, forcing the parent driving to involuntarily swerve into the parking lot. Sometimes our parents stopped in and we all got ice cream cones, and sometimes they did not. Even though I once believed my siblings and I contributed to the former destiny by leaning towards the Baskin Robbins, I'm willing to face the fact now that it was, ultimately, always Mom and Pop's call.

Women can continue to sit in the car and lean, or we can climb over into the front seat, yank the person controlling the vehicle out of the way and make a sharp-assed left into the Baskin Robbins parking lot.

This involves something I warmly refer to as:

Cuntlovin' Public Retaliation

(C.P.R. for short)

In a climate of cuntlove, if a woman in the community is raped, other women react.

We understand there is no such thing as an isolated attack on an individual woman. We understand that a Haitian-American sorority girl, a Norwegian-Filipina construction worker, a Chumash/Cree librarian or a Jewish Whore is *us*. **C.P.R.** is not at all dissimilar to a mafia philosophy in which a sister's rape is a rape of the family and cannot go unpunished. Someone has offended the honor of our family. Naturally, then, we do something about it.

In a climate of cuntlove, no one feels "lucky" it was "some other woman" who got raped. There is no such thing as "some other woman" when you have compassion and cuntlove for yourself.

The basic premise of **C.P.R.** is publicly humiliating rapists. Since rapists count on a women's shame and silence to keep them safe and on the streets, it seems to me that an undue amount of attention focused on rapists would seriously counter this assumption.

C.P.R. can be employed when a woman is sure of her attacker's identity. Since most attacks are *not* perpetrated by strangers, this is a highly relevant factor.

There is safety and power in numbers.

A group of two hundred women walking into the place of employment of a known rapist would have an effect. If each of these women were in possession of a dozen rotting eggs which were deposited onto the rapist's person, the rapist might well come to the conclusion that he had committed a very unpopular act, one that was not appreciated by the community. If a rapist had to walk through a crowd of angry, staring, silent or quietly and deadly chanting women to get to his car in the grocery store parking lot, he might feel pretty uncomfortable.

Cuntlovin' Public Retaliation has limitless possibilities.

C.P.R. actions can be executed without breaking too terribly many laws and without becoming violent—the latter being true especially if women only are present. Unnecessary violence is for stupid, unimaginative people. There are far more damaging ways to punish someone without invoking violence.

Cuntlovin' Public Retaliation serves history as well as the future. Women who have been raped may find enormous satisfaction and healing by acting out in a setting with other women who are present in total support, rage and love. In this context, we are offered a liberation from silence, self-blame, quiet acceptance or any other negative reaction we have—in the past—believed we needed for survival.

Men should not be included in **C.P.R.** actions. Excepting situations where men have been raped, the general male response towards the rape of a friend, relative or lover is outraged, self-righteous indignation. I've seen this reaction a number of times, and believe men react this way because it gives them a chance to prove to themselves what good non-raping men they are. If men really and truly want to be "good," they can stand in the background and quietly support their women friends and relatives while we stand up for ourselves. They can chip in money to charter the busses we may need to transport everyone to the **C.P.R.** site.

We don't need men to protect us.

This is between women and rapists.

More to the point, this is between women and ourselves.

Here is physics: A positive action yields a positive reaction.

At present, the cultural reaction to rape is generally a negative, shame-filled silence.

Fine, let the culture react that way.

We have the power to put something else there. Women can react in our own poetic, imaginative way, utilizing the resources in our community. We have power in numbers, and many, many means of communication.

Yes, indeedy.
It's time for a cool change.

Any rapist would feel pretty dang upset to see his car packed full with rotting fish heads and limburger cheese. Especially if it was a Jaguar XJS. Also, especially if the 542 women responsible were crowded onto the street where he lived, insisting that he move himself and his stinky car to another locale.

Nobody likes to be pelted with 2060 bloody tampons.

Wouldn't you just hate like the devil to be pilloried, smeared with dogshit, forced to kneel in front of a high-powered micro-phone on a raised platform and apologize to the ten thousand women who solemnly marched by you? Boy, that would be an unpleasant day that you might not forget right away, huh.

Perhaps some communities of women would be interested in constructing huge severed penises and burning them on a rapist's front lawn.

Cuntlovin' Public Retaliation is a valid cultural custom. Different tribes decide how to implement this custom in the community.

It could be highly effective.

Most importantly, with a little love, communication, temporary organization and networking, **Cuntlovin' Public Retaliation** is very, very possible.

It's also very, very up to you.

Part III
Reconciliation
(rĕk ən-sĭl ē-ā shən) n.

a dab of religion

Recently, I saw a lady wearing a T-shirt that read, "In the post-patriarchy, I'll be a post-feminist." I realized that just a few short years ago, our vocabulary had no need for either of these terms, and I smiled.

It was the same week nuestra Virgin Mary was on the cover of *Newsweek*. The pope is evidently receiving thousands of petitions daily from Catholics all over the globe, asking him to indoctrinate nuestra Virgin as co-redemptrix—Jesus' "equal."

Each passing day heralds the emergence of yet another athlete, rock star, activist, artist or politician who reminds women we can do pretty much whatever the fuck we want.

Signs of the dawning post-patriarchal age are positively rampant.

My 1965 Random House Dictionary reveals the following about the word "reconcile":

1. to render no longer opposed; bring to acquiescence or acceptance (usually fol. by *to*): *to reconcile someone to his* [sic] *fate*. 2. to win over to friendliness; cause to become amicable: *to reconcile hostile persons*. 3. to compose or settle (a quarrel, dispute, etc.). 4. to bring into agreement or harmony; make compatible or consistent: *to reconcile*

differing statements. 5. to reconsecrate (a desecrated church, cemetery, etc.). 6. to restore (an excommunicate or penitent) to communion in a church.

The definition most pertinent to this book is number five: "to reconsecrate a desecrated church."

The religious ritual of submerging a newborn child in a bowl of water inside a house of god is an attempt to simulate the power all women are potentially born with. If it is reasonable for the patriarchy to call these houses of god "churches," then it is reasonable for me to believe that both the individual female body and the body of womankind are churches too. *And I do.*

Fixing up our church, as well as the reference point of worship inside our hearts, is therefore a timely thing to do.

The following items comprise a church:

1. Protection from potential hostilities represented by opposing belief systems. Our mission to educate ourselves and children the way we want.

2. All mediums of art and literature depicting a corresponding creed and collective consciousness. Our immolationless stained glasses and holy scriptures that we design to our specifications.

3. Resources. Cashflow. Passing around our tithe baskets that fill our coffers with our money, honey.

For the reconciliation of our church, we will be utilizing cuntlovin' perspectives on protection, representational art and money. I start with protection because it flows nicest after the subject of rape.

Aggro Beyond Your Wildest Dreams

I will kick your fucking ass. — Ancient Goddess Mantra

Mapping Out a Belief System

The first thing you need in order to protect yourself is a womanifesto. My friend Panacea turned me on to the importance of womanifestoes when she said:

"I like them because they tell me what I think."

Defining and articulating your beliefs serves you in any context. By taking that a step further and causing those beliefs to exist in the material world, you contribute to a social climate of cuntlovin' evolution.

I offer my womanifesto on self-protection to perhaps give you some ideas about how you might write yours. A womanifesto does not have to be written. It can be a song, dance, painting or whatever medium stirs passion in your heart. I strongly suggest

creating your own womanifesto before moving on to the next
section, "Kickin' Ass Like There Ain't No Tomorrow."

The Womanifesto for the Categorical
New Freedom Lady

**when you see a really drunk girl leave a bar alone late at
night and you follow her and make sure she gets into her
taxi all right,**
that's self-protection.
**when you aren't afraid of looking like a supreme
chickenshit and ask your friend to go into a public bathroom with you because it creeps you out, but not for any
tangible reason,**
that's self-protection.
**when you are in the music store and you pick a CD by
women musicians who have your back instead of by a
bunch of boys who hog all the air time on the radio,**
that's self-protection.
**when you are sitting on the bus and the man who sits next
to you gives you a bad vibe and you get up and move to
another seat without giving a rats ass about feeling like
you're being rude,**
that's self-protection.
**when you find out which politician is supportive of women,
lesbians and motherhood and vote for her,**
that's self-protection.
**when you look at all the beautiful women on TV and in
magazines in the grocery store and think they are part of a**

weird industry run by men with major, major
dick complexes,
that's self-protection.
when you boycott all media not responsive in every way,
shape and freudian slip to women's rights,
that's self-protection.
when you make a conscious effort to spend your money in
establishments owned by women,
that's self-protection.
when you tell your dude if he can't hold his wad until you're
damn well ready to come then he's gonna hafta invest in a
strap-on dildo of your choosing,
that's self-protection.
when you ask for a raise,
that's self-protection.
when you insist everyone re-read Pippi Longstocking
again,
that's self-protection.
when you and your friends concoct plans of poetic guerrilla
terrorism against a teacher, fellow student, co-worker or
boss who sexually harasses women,
that's self-protection.
when you decide it's in your best interest to worship a
goddess who innately respects women,
that's self-protection.
when you cook a gourmet, five-course meal no one but you
will partake in,
that's self-protection.
when you "accidentally" spill your drink on a man at a

r
e
c
o
n
c
i
l
i
a
t
i
o
n

party who looks at your body rather vulpinely, and you don't
in the least appreciate it,
that's self-protection.
when you educate yourself about clitoridectomies, infibulation, forced prostitution, rape as a war tactic and a way of
controlling women, the Nation of Islam, Judaism, Chris-
tianity and prepatriarchal religions, the Inquisition,
women painters, photographers, filmmakers, poets,
writers, activists, politicians, sex-industry workers,
historians, archeologists and musicians,
that's self-protection.
when you read, then watch *The Bandit Queen,*
that's self-protection.
when you massage your friend because she's PMSing hard,
that's self-protection.
when you keep a tire iron by your front door,
that's self-protection.
when you buy a pull-up bar and install it in a doorway you
pass constantly so you end up doing pull-ups all the time,
even though you used to think you couldn't do pull-ups,
that's self-protection.
when you dance, run, jump, buy yourself a birthday cake
even though your birthday's five months away, cavort, kiss
all the girls you love to love, laugh, sing, shout, jump rope,
ding-dong ditch the house of someone who gets on your
nerves, swing, climb trees, pick your nose in public,
daydream, eat with your fingers, break something on
purpose, fart loud, skip and pin your friends to the ground
and tickle them,

that's self-protection.
every time you look in the mirror and your heart races
because you think,
"i'm so fucking rad,"
that's self-protection.
protect your self.

I wrote that when I was twenty-eight. I went through a lot of reconditioning on my own terms before I had the knowledge to sit down and compose those thoughts off the top of my head.

I grew up in a relatively small town in the Central Coast region of California. The *president of the Elks* spoke at the high school graduation ceremony I boycotted. Cruising up and down the main street in a car, going to the mall and attending drunken date-rape festivals called "parties" were the culminations of social interaction.

I was never entirely comfortable in this setting.

Until I was eighteen and left "home," I was constantly at odds with this culture I grew up in. The older I got, the more clearly I saw what was supposed to be looming ahead for me as a woman.

I wanted nothing to do with any of it.

This conflict became increasingly unsettling with each passing year. I did not want to keep my mouth shut and act ladylike, stop having sex with my girlfriends or respect the idea that all of my teachers were smarter than me. Dealing with such opposition on a day-to-day basis disrupted the momentum of womanpower I was born with. I struggled to keep my power somewhat apace with my life. This proved difficult, as I expended a large amount of energy defending my own concept of the woman I wanted to be. Furthermore, deprived of the experience I needed in order to *know* exactly what "the woman I wanted to be" *meant*, things were not only difficult, but mind-bogglingly complex as well.

At one point in my life, I detested the adage, "What does not kill me will only make me stronger."

But it is true.

When I was a kid, I was on the swim team, played tackle football and moto-mud bicycled. My friends and I endlessly plotted live-action *Charlie's Angels* episodes, including our edited-in couplings between 'Bri and Jill. Underwater Tea 'n Smash Party in the ocean always ruled. I loved the "Heidi" look and wore dresses with my waffle stompers. I was a late bloomer in terms of clearly established gender roles.

Largely through the teachings of my philandering, sexist father, who did not want me to grow up prey to men like himself, I became a premature and great advocate of vigilante-type behavior. I heartily beat the shit out of any mean boy who made the sorry mistake of pulling my pigtails or pushing any girl's face into the water fountain at school.

My mother, for obvious reasons we've already discussed, had no qualms about this sort of behavior. Fighting with girls was not cool (and seldom occurred), but she didn't give a rat's ass if I beat the shit out of a boy.

My older brother was not only bigger than all the boys at

my school, but acted in the role of sparring partner in our perpetual sibling battle for turf, rights and privileges. Childhood with my brother provided an ongoing study in the velocity of a strategically placed kick, the rhythm of a punch in the gut and the mother lode of reactions illicited from a well-timed, ear-splitting scream.

Between the (albeit dubiously inspired) sense of entitle-ment fostered by my parents' philosophies and the practical, tactical skills I derived from life with my brother—not to mention the wolf-pack mother mentality I found in such sister bad-asses as Deanna Alvarado and Hannah Class—the mean boys at my school were resoundingly pummelled whenever a girl reported untoward behavior to one of us.

A most satisfactory arrangement, as far as I was concerned.

Then I grew up.

The mean little boys who taunted and teased and harassed little girls also grew up.

We all grew up.

The taunting, teasing and harassing evolved into rape, passive-aggressive control lurking behind proclamations of "egalitarianism," sexual harassment and collective beliefs of male superiority.

I experienced damnable levels of confusion going from a little girl who accepted highly suspect gender roles to a young lady suddenly in possession of a very specific set of restrictions and scriptures.

One of the many, many, many scriptures imposed upon me once I got big, was: "It is your duty to ignore mean boys and their games."

And see, given the latitude I enjoyed throughout my early years, I just had a very difficult time ignoring this kind of stuff. But now that I was big, even if I tattled (a wimpy manipulation I rarely resorted to as a child), no one listened or cared. If I retaliated, I got in trouble, lost jobs, made enemies.

Oh, how I sometimes longed for those days on the playground when kicking a mean boy's ass was a mundane occurrence in any given school week.

It became my reality to let mean boys slide. Though I did not like it, I also didn't see much in the way of options. The operative words here are *I didn't see*. Before any option-seeing went down, I had to *really see* my own fears.

It was a *struggle* to see options.

I looked very, very painstakingly.

I came to terms with the reality that in the eyes of an overwhelming percentage of the population, my sole purpose on the planet is to make dicks ejaculate, either for procreation or recreation. Being reduced to this identity every time I venture out in public is an affront I chose to ignore for a long time. It is still a drag to see men looking at me in terms of their dicks, and to know that no matter what I accomplish as a person, or how I live my life, this will probably not change significantly in my lifetime.

If I had not avidly, passionately, relentlessly sought options, I am sure I would have gone insane. Regardless of whether or not *I* ever recognized the existence of options, they were always there. Like a faithful old family dog, my options waited for me to recover the survival skills I relinquished in adolescence.

Kicking Ass Like There Ain't No Tomorrow

It got to a point when I reasoned, if I take my survival into consideration every time I leave the sanctity of my home—if indeed, my home sometimes seems to be a fortress that deters enemy forces—then aren't I kind of like a soldier, and isn't my life kind of like a war?

It plain and simple dawned on me: Somebody here was seriously out of the loop. There was no circumventing the fact that I had allowed my nice wolf-pack mama girlhood survival skills to languish.

A sad—but certainly not irrevocable—mistake I made in order to survive into adulthood.

So let's see.

The first thing a soldier does is train. In boot camp she learns physical tactics and the psychology of her enemy. She meditates upon all the nuances that come into play in the battle of how a life lived in fear is a life half lived.

In the Army of Me, self-protection class was appointment number one, dee-dee-dun.

After I published an article about rape, a cartoonist named Ellen Forney wrote a letter to my editor. Ms. Forney eloquently pointed out my responsibility to urge women to learn how to protect ourselves, rather than merely publish essays about all the things we had to fear in this world. In the letter, Ellen described her pivotal experiences, learning and then teaching self-protection. Her letter fully inspired me. I asked if she'd be interested in teaching a class if I organized it, and she graciously agreed.

Ms. Forney taught us about using our voices and deflecting

verbal assaults before venturing into physical maneuvers. I was all geared up to kick me some ass; it was surprising to discover such a fount of strength and release simply by listening to women talk about how we deal with everyday situations that rankle the psyche in a slow and eroding process.

I learned a lot of physical tactics in this first self-protection class. More importantly, it became clear that these skills exist as part of a larger philosophy of self-protection that is explored and practiced by each individual woman, on our terms, at our pace.

Ellen's class ruled, and my second self-protection class kept the ol' synapse pulsations spurring along.

The next course I took was Model Mugging. It's a form of self-protection developed by a group of martial arts experts. A woman in this group had been raped. This, in itself, is not terribly unique. However, she was an eighth-degree karate black belt. She knew a martial art very, very well, but she did not know how to protect herself in the specific context of sexual assault. The group decided to pool their expertise and design a way to teach any woman, regardless of agility, prowess or strength, to protect herself.

They did an awesome, good job.

Model Mugging was intensive and expensive, and all my ass-kickin' dreams came true because there were *actual, live human men* in padded outfits that I got to pound on. My job in this class was to use my power to change the physical course of another human being who, for all intents and purposes, meant me harm. Even though I was in a room with nineteen other women and rubber mats were spread out all over the floor, the reality was daunting. *These men were present to attack and react.*

Us twenty women were present to react and attack.

Attack, attack, react, react over and over and over.

Certainly on par with the joy of actually downing the big, burly, padded dudes was watching other women negotiate power against them. This was when I *really understood* there are as many different definitions for self-protection as there are cerebral filing systems. No one reacted to the exact same situation in the exact same way, even though we were all being taught the exact same tactics.

A womanifesto and self-protection classes (note the plural form of "class") are fantastic starting points for powerful reconditioning. Define what you believe. Train your mind and body to react to detrimental situations in a powerful, assertive way. These two survival tactics are, however, just that: *tactics*. They *help* your brain to think differently.

Remember back yonder when I induced an abortion without going to the vacuum cleaner? Remember how the herbs I took aided me in directing *my own focus?* The same concept holds true here (and at many other outposts in a cuntlovin' lady's life). Training requirements aren't fulfilled by attending a course every Wednesday night for eight weeks. Self-protection is a *way of thinking, constantly,* each and every moment of your life. Classes help. Entertaining pro-active dialogues with the women you love helps. Womanifestoes help. Lotsa stuff helps. *Nothing* is as valuable as implementing new learning tools and committing to your focus for *the rest of your life.*

I advocate self-protection as a lifestyle philosophy-modus operandi. I don't believe that wielding a can of pepper spray, a switchblade or a gun is on par with existing on the planet with a self-protection lifestyle at the forefront of one's being.

Neither do I in any way oppose the use of weapons as self-protection. When one chooses weapons to protect oneself in this world, it is of *utmost importance* to learn *formal, rigorous safety and precision in the specific context of protection from physical and/or sexual assault.* Deer hunting and gang banging are probably not gonna prepare your spirit, mind or body for a potential sexual assault.

The most reliable weapon is your mind. When women relinquish the power of our minds to objects that can inflict debilitating pain or death, we weaken our position. A quick, resourceful, well-trained thinker is a *much deadlier opponent* than someone who projects power into a deadly instrument.

A quick, resourceful, well-trained thinker with a deadly instrument in hand is then Warrior Goddess incarnate.

Hee fucken hawww.

Cross that bridge when you get to it.

In the meantime, the most wonderful way I have found to train my mind for assessing situations and reacting with the resources I have available to me is on a checkered playing board that has two sets of sixteen figurines carved to represent different qualities and nuances of power.

Chess Is Our Friend

I am thankful to Boaz Yakim, a gentleman who made a movie I will watch any time, any place. It's called *Fresh.* In light of its *phenomenal* importance, the injustice of *Fresh*'s poor distribution makes me almost pass out.

Fresh is an adolescent young man growing up in a situation rife with predators. His environment is predatory, his inherited socioeconomic latitude is a predator and all but one of his role models are predators. Fresh's sole nonpredatory role model is his father, played by the incomparable Mr. Samuel L. Jackson.

Fresh lives in a foster home. He isn't supposed to see his father, but he does. Every week, they play chess together in a park. I said Fresh's father is not a predator, but that's not altogether true. He manifests his predatory traits on the chessboard, in the game he lives and breathes by.

The story of Fresh unfolds around these weekly chess games with his father. Territory being what it is, both on the chess board and in life, Fresh's father routinely wins the game. Meanwhile, in his day-to-day life (of which his father is completely ignorant), Fresh faces responsibilites and situations that would cause chronic intestinal complications to the heartiest CEO at IBM.

Fresh meets his father in the park every week and plays this very old game. It is kind of a ritual. His father says things like, "What kind of player am I? Am I an offensive player or a defensive player? Right, I'm neither. *I play my opponent.*"

With all his heart, Fresh listens, looks, learns. The gift of chess and its lessons in strategy may be all his estranged, alcoholic father has to offer him. It is also more valuable than an eight-digit trust fund.

Fortified with nothing more than a psychology that assesses and undermines their *individual* ways of operating, Fresh pretty much mauls every predator in his life—without personally committing a single act of violence. He learns how to *think like the predators*. You know who reigns supreme, or the movie wouldn't be called *Fresh*.

Fresh has become one of the biggest role models in my life. I constantly ask myself, "How would Fresh deal with this situation?" When I'm reacting like a dork in response to some damn stimuli or another, I say, "Fresh wouldn't do that in a million years." Perhaps most significantly, Fresh reminds me to get off my ass and play chess every chance I get.

My father taught me how to play chess when I was five. I played quite often with my sparring partner—er, brother. Just as I had grown up and left my survival skills in the hinterland, I likewise stopped playing chess at some obscure point in adolescence. Whenever I had the opportunity to play chess as an adult, I met a fierce resistance inside myself. I didn't like the competetion, the cutthroat vibe.

After Fresh came into my life, I managed to shred this resistance asunder. However, it turned out most of my opponents were of the male persuasion. With precious few exceptions, my girl friends either never learned how to play or said the same thing I always said, "I used to play when I was younger, but I haven't played in a long time." As if not having played "in a long time" is somehow grounds for continuing this trend. Throughout my non-chess-playing rehabilitation, this response started sounding like, "I used to enjoy honing my strategy and getting what I want by employing my vast intelligence, but that stuff just doesn't interest me anymore."

Chess is a psychological exercise. It whets the brain for every conceivable means of self-protection.

When my pieces are threatened, my brain is presented with a puzzle. I must come up with a way to counter—with a ruse, sacrifice or threat of my own. No apologies. My A-1 priority is devising any plan in the whole wide world that does not involve retreat. Unless it diverts my opponent's attention from how devastatingly I plan to fuck them over on my next coupla moves, retreat is an absolute anathema.

Each person I play chess with tells me about their way of surviving in the world. If I piece together an overall view of their modus operandi, I win. When I sit across the board from someone, I'm engaged in more than a game. I silently beseech, "Tell me how you survive." Each opponent I play offers yet another survival strategy for my cerebral filing system.

Chess teaches how to deal with threatening situations and individuals *in the midst* of taking territory for oneself. The chances of being caught off guard have discernable boundaries. Predators become opponents instead of scary monsters over whom one has no control. When played on a regular basis, chess melds into one's consciousness. It becomes evident that one is never not playing this game.

Chess fortifies the psyche. When interwoven with physical and psychological training, it keeps a lady on her self-protective toes.

This game matters.

Get good at it and then get better.

Play chess with your friends instead of watching the M TeeVee. Organize all-girl tournaments at your school and all-women tournaments at your work. If you're not kickin' everybody's butt, then put a lot of thought into why they're kickin' yours. Play yourself. Play your mom. Invite a woman you think you can't stand to play a game with you. Play chess at a coffee house with someone you would never otherwise interact with. Have e-mail chess challenges. Tell your boss if you beat her at chess she hasta give you a raise.

Get on down and get back up again.

Play chess every day.

Predators Are Our Friends

I founded a direct-action anti-rape warfare group called Mobilizing Our Neighbors and Sisters To Eradicate Rape (M.O.N.S.T.E.R.). More accurately, I thought up a clever acronym and organized a space for women to come together and address the issue of rape as a cultural oppression tactic used to control women. The group of women involved did all the founding.

M.O.N.S.T.E.R.'s objective, decided upon after much discussion and debate, was to be a primarily nonviolent vigilante group that (more or less poetically) terrorized known sexual predators in our community, educated people about rape and provided a safe, supportive environment for women to devise and carry out nefarious plans of poetic attack.

As with every activist group on the planet, M.O.N.S.T.E.R. consisted of a balance of two creeds. One was of the passive leaflet-plastering, networking persuasion, while the other had a much more aggressive, predatory nature.

For many weeks, I interacted with this group of bright, imaginative, angry women and listened carefully to both systems of belief. While I was a subscriber to the predatory creed, I came to have a deep understanding of the women who wanted to act out in a more genteel manner. The argument ran along the lines of "We don't want to act like predators because then we are lowering ourselves to the level of a rapist," which is as valid an argument as can possibly be. This would invariably provoke the "nature vs. nuture" argument and someone would cite the ferocity of a mother serengeti lion or an arctic mama polar bear.

As is evidenced by M.O.N.S.T.E.R.'s eventual objectives, compromises were reached, leaning towards the predatory.

What I learned from this experience was a pretty solid foundation for *Cunt:* When women 100 percent define anything—from simple words to complex institutions—the meaning or outcome inherently serves us *most* satisfactorily. Period.

It is very simple, but a lot of work.

A predator, as defined by our society, is a bad man who will hurt you.

Ouch.

A predator, as defined by M.O.N.S.T.E.R., is a nice lady who pro-actively protects herself and the women in her community.

Whee!

Both definitions are sound.

M.O.N.S.T.E.R.'s cuntlovin' definition doesn't attempt to make the former one null and void. It sits right along next to it, happy as the day is long. Practically *the instant* we actually defined "predator" for ourselves, the group's Kali the Destroyers piped down a few notches, while nuestra Virgens de Guadalupe started baring teeth.

Fucken refreshing, you know?

201

❋

Predators are important people. Why else would there be one in almost every movie and story throughout history. Take away the predator, and where does that leave the koran, bible, torah?

Nowhere, that's where.

Predators are not the problem.

I, for one, don't *feel* like going out into the world and making sure all the predators who focus on women are put behind bars or executed or whatever. In this cuntfearing society, there's plenty more where that came from. Some Sisyphean tasks can be fun, but that's not one of them.

It is impossible to change the fact that sexual predators are a product of our society, whether they are incarcerated or free to roam. And *damn,* it sucks that no incantation from heaven and hell combined will undo the deeply rooted damage rape has already done to the collective consciousness of womankind.

Dang, that's all impossible, so forget it.

Say goodbye to the impossible: toodle doo.

It *is* possible to change our way of reacting and dealing. Without silence, the *cycle*, the *livelihood* of violence towards women goes hectic. Women break the cycle and the situation then belongs to us.

Our ball, our court, our move.

As I see it, the major problem facing us ladies is not all the horrible shit that's been happening to us for the past two thousand–odd years.

Nor is it the perpetrators of the horrible shit.

The problem is we don't seem to think we have much of a

predatory disposition. This is heartily reinforced by our culture, which unduly punishes women who are caught acting out in a violent, predatory way. It frightens people very, very much when women do violent things. The United States legal and judicial systems are hardly exempt from this fear. Jails are populated with women who murdered the lovers, friends or male relatives who assaulted us or our children for years. If it is at all possible to completely avoid contact with this sector of society, I suggest doing so with vigor.

Physical violence is something one resorts to only when it is the very, very, very best way to safety. Violence is not a defining trait of a lady predator. It is certainly imperative to know how, when, why and where to be violent. It is also imperative to know how, when, why and where to get away before a situation has the chance to escalate.

Lady predators are cuntlovin', imaginative women. We therefore manifest our predatory stance in just such a manner. We're not too shy to be highly visible. We'll scream "My Country 'Tis of Thee" to drown the voice of Loudmouth Asshole who is trying to impress his friends by telling everyone on the street the effect we do/do not have on his dick. We're not too proud to be invisible, either. We know that for Mr. Obviously Fucked Up in the Head, "Amazing Grace" sung soft 'n low under our breath miraculously makes him forget we're crossing his path.

Lady predators get all our friends to confront the dickwad who bugs us at work or school. We ensure employers know which of their employees is a date rapist and picket the place if

c
u
n
t

the boss does not respond accordingly. We publicly humiliate
the man who rapes our daughter, sister, lover, mother. We
organize into mama wolf packs with a rabid sense of humor.
We have Abusive Husband Treasure Hunts on Super Bowl
Sunday.

We interrupt the game.

It

is

funner 'n shit.

Who Remedios Varo Is

If you would understand a people, look at them through the eyes of the poet, the musician and the artist.

—Cynthia Pearl Maus, *The World's Great Madonnas*

When I was ten, the Fam took a trip to L.A. to see the Treasures of King Tut exhibit. At this time, my art world consisted of paintings, pictures, books, records and the radio. (My father's tyranny is in evidence here. We didn't have a television set in our house for *simply ages.*) Art was furthermore associated with making a huge mess that was magically sanctioned by most all authority figures.

Art was a wonder to perceive, and I percieved it at complete and utter face value. This is to say, I very much enjoyed art, but did not attach a symbolic interpretation to either my own or other people's.

The King Tut exhibit forever altered this tabula rasa.

I remember gold.

I remember gold, and I remember four women who

guarded the box where King Tut's body lay. They were gold, of course, and stood with arms to their sides, hands outstretched hip high, palms perfectly at my eye level, staring me down. Their eyes never left anyone in the room. They saw all. They were impassable. Their gaze was searing and irresistible, like licking a nine-volt battery.

My parents and siblings wandered off. I was not interested in anything else the King Tut exhibit had to offer, and installed myself with the sentinels until it was time to go.

I knew little of Christ, much less anything that went on Before Christ, but it was quite obvious those sentinels were *obscenely* out of their element in a museum in Los Angeles, California, circa One Thousand Nine Hundred and Seventy Whatever A.D. And yet—through what I later recognized as the wanton pillage mentality of my culture—in this context, innocu-ously referred to as "archeology"—there they irrefutably stood.

Magnificent overseers of an entire civilization, brought across oceans on a boat driven by the victors of history's present telling.

I felt incredibly minute and *of the flesh* in their presence. It was important to remain in contact with what was in the pocket of my shorts: half a bag of M&M's and two green plastic army men I'd fished out of my little brother's mouth on the drive to L.A. I think the contents of my pockets comforted me, because fear was certainly present.

The sentinels possessed incomprehensible powers for thousands upon thousands of years. They were *alive* under the desert sands of Egypt long before even my *grammy* was born. And now, standing in this weird museum room, they were not only alive, but *pissed as hell* to be taken from their place.

I could not stop digging the amazement of this whole situation.

I was too young and impatient to understand what compelled people to create all that gold stuff, and too uninterested in the museum itself to put much thought into the little explanatory plaques affixed near each piece, but I knew God when I saw Her.

This, I understood.

This, I respected.

This was a whole new slant on art.

I grew up and found out three more things about art:

1. The individual artist is a *medium* for making representational and deeply meaningful symbols of the community's collective consiousness, whether they are symbols of the community's religion, love, hurt, power, hate, hope, dreams, fables, foibles or on and on and on.

2. Some cultures know this, think it's divine, and respect the importance of art and artists as perfectly natural manifestations of innate human life, growth and expression—without insanely glorifying huge, corporate-induced false images of individual superstars.

3. American culture is not one of them.

One kind of art occurs naturally in the course of everyday life, and does not generally involve widespread cultural glorification. My mother's Thanksgiving dinner is art. The one Aunt Genie creates is of a completely different genre, though she utilizes the same basic components. The dashboard of Liz's car is art. Shells and goddesses and pretty rocks are arranged in a specific way that holds meaning for anyone who is privy to the need for protection when navigating an automobile. Grammy's wildflower and bird sanctuary garden is art. She designed it. It is a reflection of her and her community. It is symbolic of the culture she lives in.

Another kind of art is the art people make and *intend* to be considered art as symbolic representation. Art such as this moves you for certain very specific reasons directly related to your history and experiences, and moves your girlfriend in a thousand and one absolutely different ways.

This art includes paintings, metal work, sculptures, murals, photographs, dances, poems, stories, storytelling, essays, plays, screenplays, movies, videos, ads, buildings, fashion designs, performances, puppet shows, monuments, pornography, erotica, music, spoken word and so on.

Both kinds of art represent a culture, a collective consciousness and the passions of an individual. Grammy's wildflower and bird sanctuary garden is as monumental as Toni Morrison's epic, *Beloved*.

On a scale that measured love and pain,
they'd proportionately weigh the same.

The difference between these two kinds of art is:

I know my grammy's story and the average onlooker does not. I've developed an emotional bond with my grammy since I was born. Therefore, I walk into her garden equipped with a lifelong perception which is in continual evolution. I am thus able to identify with her garden utilizing symbolism unavailable to most everyone else.

Beloved directly, out and out tells a story. The words of the story are arranged with high regard for the common bond of human-ness that each and every reader shares. Everyone who can read is equipped to identify with *Beloved*.

Beloved taps into the collective consciousness of a community that spans the entire planet.

Grammy's garden doesn't echo out much farther than Sweet Home, Oregon.

Art imitates life as life imitates art. Art and the community are whirling dervishes unto one other. Takes two to tango. It doesn't matter which one causes and affects the other, or when, or why, or how. This came first: the chicken or the egg.

There is, of course, a huge problem here.

Throughout the history of Western civilization—and by this term, I mean the destructive, competitive, capitalist, patriarchal, filthy-rich, white, male social system which threatens to consume every other culture on the planet—what is considered "art" has been presented by and for far less than half of the human community: the white, male portion. Art that our culture takes seriously, invests in and reflects upon was created by men. Women do not belong to the "art" community, as it presently exists.

In what is considered the art community, the enormous contributions of artists such as Yoko Ono and Octavia Butler are methodically and unquestionably overshadowed by those of the Andy Warhol/Stephen King ilk.

In the early '90s, I attended college at one of America's most *liberal, progressive* institutions. There, my friend Panacea turned me on to the surrealist painter, Remedios Varo.

One quarter, Panacea took a course in "art history." She asked her teacher numerous times throughout the quarter to include Ms. Varo's totally brilliant, fabulous and inspiring work in the program. The teacher resolutely overruled this motion, time and again. His argument was that there must be a solid reason why Ms. Varo's work was not "good enough" to be included in any of the art history books he had ever seen. Since none of the sources this teacher deemed reputable recognized Remedios Varo, why on earth should he?

Catch-22, deedle dee-doo.

In her second autobiography, *Beyond the Flower*, Judy Chicago provides a simple, astute answer:

> Historically, women have either been excluded from the process of creating the definitions of what is considered art or allowed to participate only if we accept and work within existing mainstream designations. If women have no real role *as women* in the process of defining art, then we are essentially prevented from helping to shape cultural symbols. (Chicago, 1996, 72)

As I learned in a beautiful book entitled *Spider Woman's Granddaughters*, there is a name for this: intellectual apartheid. In her brilliant introduction to *Spider Woman's Granddaughters*, Paula Gunn Allen speaks as a Native artist working in the white-American literary world, but her profound truth is applicable to many artists existing in many worlds:

Intellectual apartheid . . . helps create and maintain political apartheid; it tends to manifest itself in the practical affairs of all societies that subscribe to it. Contrary to popular and much scholarly opinion in Western intellectual circles, aesthetics are not extraneous to politics. And because political conquest necessarily involves intellectual conquest, educational institutions in this country have prevented people from studying the great works of minority cultures in light of critical structures that could illuminate and clarify those materials in their own contexts. The literatures and arts of non-Western peoples have thus remained obscure to people educated in Western intellectual modes. Moreover, non-Western literature and art appear quaint, primitive, confused, and unworthy of serious critical attention largely because they are presented that way. (Allen, 1989, 3)

Men forge merrily along, continuing to get 99.9 percent of the credit for doing pretty much everything. When the glaringly obvious retardation of this situation is pointed out, the ensuing rebuttal tends to be that men just unanimously happen to be the most fabulously talented creators on earth. Thus, everyone who is not a man fails to get due credit.

In order for women painters, for instance, to be included in the history of art in modern civilization, it must first of all be established that we *exist*. This places the art work *in the hinterland* of the artist's gender. Women artists are required to explain our presence, to defend our identity, to speak for our multitudes, and men are not.

Meanwhile, reproduction upon reproduction of women in various stages of undress litters "art history." Women artists are airbrushed out of art history and still endure alienation and invalidation, yet images of women positively abound as the focal point of men's art work.

In this kind of setting, one learns that Salvador Dali is deemed an uncontested surrealist Master (though he readily admitted his obsessive reliance on a woman named Galarina for inspiration), while you probably don't know who I am talking about when I name a chapter for Remedios Varo, one of the most freaking genius surrealists of the twentieth century, who relied on herself for just about everything.

In 1989, the Guerrilla Girls—a pro-activist group that will be discussed at length in just a few short pages—addressed the question, "Do women have to be naked to get into the Metropolitan Museum?" Here are their findings:

> Asked to design a billboard for the Public Art Fund [PAF] in New York [City], we welcomed the chance to do something that would appeal to a general audience. One Sunday morning we conducted a "weenie count" at the Metropolitan Museum of Art in New York, comparing the number of nude males to nude females in the artworks on display. The results were very "revealing." (Guerrilla Girls, 1995, 61)

They designed a billboard depicting a reproduction of Ingres's reclining *Odalisque*, with a gorilla mask on her head and a dildo in the hand draped over her hip. Accompanying this image was the following statement: "Less than 5 percent of the artists in the Modern Art Sections are women, but 85 percent of the nudes are female."

Alas, the Public Art Fund and the Guerrilla Girl's *Odalisque* were not meant for each other.

> The PAF said our design wasn't clear enough and rejected
> it. We then rented advertising space on NYC busses and
> ran it ourselves, until the bus company canceled our lease,
> saying the image . . . was too suggestive and that the figure
> appeared to have more than a fan in her hand. (Guerrilla
> Girls, 1995, 61)

The difficulty in locating art made by women artists compared with the *impossibility* of avoiding art work created by men reflects *how women live* in this culture.

It is the absolute normal reality.

Cultural symbols that hold deep representational meaning for the community are shaped by the victors of history's present telling. The victors have a time-tested interest in controlling women's bodies, decimating civilizations, playing cops and robbers, keeping people of color and white women in our "proper" pigeonholed place and glorifying themselves through power plays with each other.

These interests are serviced through most television shows, movies, songs and music videos readily available. The interests of the victors project and reinforce absolutely *nada, zilch, nothing, zero,* that serves women.

Yet we view and absorb this art every livelong day.

c
u
n
t

And it hurts us.

Ouch.

Every day.

Here is a paragraph from the 1997 handbook for the Michigan Womyn's Music Festival:

> If you play recorded music that can be heard by others, please make it music with womyn only vocals. We come here to enjoy a womyn-only environment, part of which is hearing only womyn's voices. This is not a judgment on men or music, but a strong, positive desire to spend these few special days surrounded only by the sounds of womyn.

The Michigan Womyn's Music Festival is an unparalleled spiritual experience for—I'd be willing to wager—every woman who attends. It is a weeklong world created not so much without men, as with women. Women cook the food, play the music, guard the gates and drive the shuttle busses twenty-four hours a day. We see, speak, smell, taste and touch nothing but women. Every structure, artifact and song is of women's creation. It is not often one has the opportunity to exist in an entire community of women, wholly untouched by men, even for a day.

The only men who set foot on the festival grounds do so to empty out the Porta-Janes.

It can change a lady forever.

When I step outside my home, I am besieged by the creations of men. They designed the cars driving down the streets, indeed, they planned the placement of the streets. Since architecture is one of the many, many fields considered "male dominated," I trust that most of the buildings and residences I see come from the blueprints of men's minds. Ditto landscaping. The probably male-designed movie posters at the bus stops usually feature men, and if not, represent the labor of male producers, directors, sound engineers and camera operators. If I turn on the radio while I am driving down this male-made street, the voices of men selling their products and singing their songs about how much they love/hate/want to fuck women will promenade into into my male-designed automobile.

It is not difficult to appreciate the art of men.

In fact, it is dang-ola a chore to altogether evade it.

For two years in college, I read only books by women. I did not watch television or read magazines in the check-out line. I studied paintings, photographs, sculptures and films created solely by women.

George Bush got hisself inaugurated, Ted Bundy counted down the days to his execution and Somalia cried out in pain, but I was in Zora Neale Hurston's world. Leslie Marmon Silko kissed me good night. Sister Rosetta Tharpe sang lullabies into my sleep. Diane Arbus scared me giddy. Maya Linn was the Cinderella of my heart. Käthe Kollowitz made me cry and cry and cry.

It was only an experiment. I only meant it to be one of those let's-see-what-happens-if-I-do-this kind of things. But it turned into sort of a habit. I fully immersed myself in the expressions of women, exclusively, and felt so comfortable, I guess I just didn't leave.

I wouldn't venture to advocate a supreme, *lifelong* militancy about the gender specifics of art appreciation. I recently finished Laurence Leamer's eight hundred–plus page book, *The Kennedy Women: The Saga of an American Family*. Chet Baker croons through the speakers as I write. The taxidermy manual I read last month was written by a man, but I've forgotten his name, Jesse Charles or something. As far as I'm concerned, Samuel L. Jackson is a demigod and I'm neverendingly inspired by the garden of Mr. Young-Park, who lives next door.

It's not a bad idea, however, to focus *solely* on the artistic expressions of women for *at least* one year. That way you notice not only the horrifying prevalence of male artistic expression much more, but the mother lode of inspiration and brilliance our grandmothers, mothers and sisters have produced.

I loathe special sections for women just as much as the next lady. It will forever bug the shit out of me that there's a "W" before "NBA." This designation makes certain we know that all basketball involves men, unless it's this special, *exceptional circumstance* which can only be qualified as "women's basketball."

Schools have classes called "women's studies," and "African-American literature" because the standard for *existence* set by white men has yet to be rescinded in this age. "Normal" history is the history of a certain class of white people, from the perspective of men. All the other histories are precisely that: other.

I wish that when I said "rockstar," the kneejerk status quo association was Me'Shell "Brilliant Goddess Lovechild" NdegéOcello instead of Keith "Piece of Shit" Richards.

I wish when I queried "Great American Writer?" most people standing on the street would respond, "Oh, yes, well *obviously* Flannery O'Connor and Louise Erdrich," instead of, "Why, John Steinbeck and Ernest Hemingway, of course."

But that is not the case at all.

There is subsequently an unfortunate—yet urgent—need for something I'll refer to as a "Cuntlovin' Women's Art Movement." At least, until our culture no longer recognizes women within a male paradigm, and language and perception have broadened enough to imply the [art] world's inclusion of and dependence upon women.

Also, not to sound like a total wet blanket.

The *multitude* of acclaimed cuntlovin' artists bustin' fine round womanly asses getting honest reflections of us into the world *thrills me beyond measure.* Women populate the stages, giving acceptance speeches for Nobels, Grammys, Pulitzers and Guggenheims like never before. With each passing year, it grows easier and easier to immerse oneself in the expressions of women.

The singular detail here is to *immerse* yourself in the expressions of women; to *create* a Cuntlovin' Women's Art Movement with your friends, sisters, lovers and daughters; to be part of the community that defines art.

r
e
c
o
n
c
i
l
i
a
t
i
o
n

Cuntlovin' Women's Art Movement

Item #C.W.A.M.-1: chant

> You are what you eat.
> You meet who you greet.
> You head where you tread.
> You dead when not fed.

Cuntlovin' Women's Art Movement

Item #C.W.A.M.-2: womanifesto

the neverending "she taught me" womanifesto

. . . diamanda galás.

she taught me.

all the pain and joy of the whole wide world is inside my body.

my dna never forgets.

her voice in my body is the inquisition, all slavery ever, all rape,

all war, AIDS. her voice brings all that pain into my body—

which hurts—but the fact that she offers me the opportunity to

physically perceive the complexities of this pain, which exists in

the world in her voice, means it exists in the world in my body,

too. knowing this, the ball's in my court to take responsibility,

which gives me power.

all the pain and joy of the whole wide world is inside my body.

my dna never forgets.

leslie marmon silko.

she taught me.

if i want it to, history can mean his story. but mostly and much

moreover, history means

hi, story.

she said hi, story, and i understood what the vietnam war was

from her perspective, which mirrors my own much more

closely than the textbooks i read in school. she told me cowboys

and indians are people i see in my everyday life, the *nahual* flies

overhead, slavery is a business based on male sexuality and

home is where the heart is.

if i want it to, history can mean his story. but mostly and much

moreover, history means

hi, story.

pippi longstocking.

she taught me.

don't you worry about me, i always come out on top.

she reigns supreme over the police, mean boys, pirates, nosey

parkers, uppity snoots, the education system, monsters and

rascally impositions of her culture. the wonders of just simply

being alive in the world are limited solely by her imagination.

she was one of the first fashion inspirations of my life, and when i

grew up, her stories became the vortex of my feminist rhetoric.

don't you worry about me, i always come out on top.

remedios varo.

she taught me.

i am what i eat.

she painted pictures of magic happening, which are also what

her paintings, themselves, are. her life, her cosmology and her

c
u
n
t

product are three mirrors peering into one another at the same time, infinity. her precise science is based on the findings deep inside her consciousness and it is irrefutable. what comes from her is what she is because she is what she comes from.

i am what i eat. . . .

Cuntlovin' Women's Art Movement
Item #C.W.A.M.-3: http://www.guerrillagirls.com

The Guerrilla Girls have been an exemplary part of this culture for over a decade. Here is their mission statement:

> The Guerrilla Girls are a group of women artists and arts professionals who make posters about discrimination. Dubbing ourselves the conscience of the art world, we declare ourselves feminist counterparts to the mostly male tradition of anonymous do-gooders like Robin Hood, Batman, and the Lone Ranger. We wear gorilla masks to focus on the issues rather than our personalities. We use humor to convey information, provoke discussion, and show that feminists can be funny. In 10 years, we have produced over 70 posters, printed projects, and actions that expose sexism and racism in the art world and the culture at large. Our work has been passed around the world by kindred spirits who consider themselves Guerrilla Girls too. The mystery surrounding our identities has attracted attention and support. We could be anyone; we are every-where. (www.guerrillagirls.com)

The Guerrilla Girls are one of the most internationally recognized activist groups on the planet. Though they'll never get due credit, the Guerrilla Girls' poster style is a huge inspirational prototype for the strong-image/in-your-face text combo that has become formulaic in everything from Nike ads to blockbuster movie trailers.

Their tactics are clever, humorous and highly effective. They attack specific issues at specific locations. Guerrilla Girl propaganda is clearly and concisely worded. The vivid, often co-opted images grab the attention of non-English-speaking people, those unable to read and the completely jaded, alike.

Were the Guerrilla Girls originally a bunch of seventeen-year-old kids who bullshitted a mission statement into being, got their act together and poetically terrorized the art world after they finished their homework every afternoon?

Are the Guerrilla Girls really a smattering of disgruntled career gals who realized how very, very pissed off they were that they had "sold out" instead of pursuing their passions as artists?

Are Chelsea and Hillary Clinton Guerrilla Girls?

How weird must it be for men who work with women in New York's finest museums and galleries *not to know* if one of their colleagues, bosses or subordinates is one of an increasingly powerful group of women who undermine everything they allegedly work towards together during business hours?

It is very delicious that so much surrounding this group is a matter of conjecture.

Here's a conservative guess:

The Guerrilla Girls originated as seven to twenty-eight

women who decided to do something together instead of sitting
back and witnessing the horror.

Talk about an inspiration to the nation.

Here is the recipe for starting an activist group in your
hometown:

a. pictures

b. words

c. a reproduction and distribution system

d. women friends with imagination, focus and motiva-
tion—especially ones who work at Kinko's.

Put it all together.

On your marks,

get set.

Go.

Cuntlovin' Women's Art Movement
Item #C.W.A.M.-4: disbursement of revenue

Get CDs and books at the library when appreciating the work
of men. Rent their movies. Watch their sporting events on TV.

Buy CDs and books by women. Go to the theater to see
films by women, and purchase videos for your gorgeously
expanding library. Buy tickets to our basketball games.

Disburse revenue into the women's art world in your
community and afar. Each cent spent on work by men is money
taken away from the Cuntlovin' Women's Art Movement.

Who Mammon Is

The ceiling isn't glass, it's a very dense layer of men.
—Anne Jardim

 I love money.
I love money so much I can hardly contain my passion for it.

Money rules.

Besides shelter, featuring a warm cushy bed, heat, electricity, a pot to piss in and a floor to watch my period blood drip onto, money equals: time to work on my book, presents for people I love, a sumptuous, satin-lined, floor-length, pink, polyester fur coat with matching bikini, mango mochi ice cream, a telephone line and an e-mail account, a three hour luxuriation and massage at the communal women's baths, new books and CDs, industrial-sized rolls of double-sided tape, sheets of stickers with my face next to an alien's, fancy dinner dates and that divine three tiered cocktail table at the antique store.

Lordisa yes, money is grand.

Making,

managing and

generating

yet more money in a cuntlovin' way that makes me smile from earlobe to earlobe is an absolute different story.

There are two ways to make money in a capitalist, patriarchal setting:

1. Fuck other people over faster and more efficiently than they fuck you over.
2. Whore.

I'm too much of a sucker for the wrath of karma to excel at #1, so that leaves #2. In this context, Whoring consists of selling some aspect of one's being in order to survive. Sometimes this is selling one's dexterity at the espresso machine and other times it's selling one's ability to seduce people into buying things they don't want. Sometimes we think we can escape corporate Whoredom by becoming artists or owning our own businesses.

But no.

To make money, we gotta associate ourselves with a corporate pimp somewhere along the food chain.

This ain't circumventable.

Any kind of Cuntlovin' Women's Economic System that's implemented in this society will have to answer to the capitalist patriarchy because the buck stops there. It is downright illegal to ignore the IRS. Please inform me if there's a single behemoth insurance company owned and operated by women, but I'm quite certain the New York Stock Exchange floor has never been grid-locked by cuntlovin' ladies vying to invest in the education of our children.

So be it.

At the 1997 Michigan Womyn's Music Festival, I met a writer for a popular American magazine. We got to talking, and duly realized that we totally disagreed on pretty much every mien of existence. This in no way hampered our mutual fascination and respect for one another.

I will never in my life forget her candor when she said to me (of all people) in an unabashedly woman-centered community (of all places), "I am totally seduced by male power."

In context, it was one of the most brutally honest statements I'd ever heard—even though (and indubitably because) I could not relate on any spectrum of cognizance. She'd put great and highly intelligent thought into her choice for survival, which involved investing all of her power and trust in the capitalist patriarchy economic model.

Which makes perfect sense.

The proof is in the pudding.

The largest, most successful women-owned companies in the United States are cute little unicorns that play in the rainbow compared to the village-stomping dragons like Microsoft, GE and Disney.

I ain't never heard tell of an internationally recognized multimedia production company, chain of car dealerships, real estate conglomerate, advertising agency or garbage-collection firm owned and operated solely by women. There are no states with women in all positions of political office, from the governor on down to the postmaster in each city. If mafias are needed to keep the economy humming along, there certainly aren't any matrifocal ones testifying to the truth of this.

This has been the economic reality since time out of my grammy's mind. Past and present cuntlovin' businesses are inherently at odds in this reality. Subsequently, they must fight like the devil in order to remain solvent.

Cunt would never have become a product accessible to consumers if it weren't for the rippling effect of one woman's struggle and tenacious dream. One woman's unwavering standard to employ and serve women creates a cuntlovin' consciousness that bolsters every person who works for—or comes in contact with—her company. Rest assured, pretty much any product purchased from a cuntlovin' business benefits all women in a similar manner.

Cuntlovin' businesswomen are consistently on the economic defense because—at present—we aren't the ones who foment the rules and codes of supply and demand. Women have no modern history of managing commerce on the civic, county, state or federal level.

I am a sharecropper on the patriarchy's land.

I can dress this up with all the modes of independence imaginable, but if I want my mail every day, I am at the mercy of the United States Postal Service. The electricity for my computer is compliments of the Pacific Gas and Electric Company, which still often boasts repair signs that remind me of the fact that this society is run by a series of "Men Working."

Furthermore, individual women are systematically shot down when we make a stand in the name of anything that defies the white male standard of existence. To my dying day, I'm gonna be cranky about the fact that Dr. Jocelyn Elders got canned for testing our society's puritanical tolerance level about sexuality.

Women who acquire the courage, will and/or money to secure positions of high-octane power and prestige *must conduct business* within the same "mainstream designations" found in the art world. Likewise, in order to become and remain a hugely successful organization, woman-owned companies must alienate women.

Marjorie Merriweather Post, for example.

Her father, C. W. Post, of Raisin Bran fame, was right there at the crest of the breakfast and advertising economic revolutions here in America. He insisted his only child be involved in the intrigues of business. Marjorie was raised much differently than other girls of her generation. She grew up with a sense of entitlement and independence, believing her gender was certainly no hindrance in getting what she wanted. Undoubtedly, this is more a reflection of C. W. Post's money, whiteness and love for his only child, than the philosophies of the women's movement at the time. The result was, nonetheless, a strong-willed woman who controlled a huge corporation after her father kicked. Almost until the day she died, Ms. Post ran the family business, and she did so under the same model as every other "successful" corporation in America. Men held positions of power and decision. Women were secretarial mom-wife-Whore-sis sycophants.

I reckon if the breakfast-cereal industry hadn't been revolutionized by C. W. Post and the Kellogg brothers until, oh say 1960, and Marjorie Merriweather Post was raised in the '70s and took over in the '90s, Post Cereal would've ran its course along pretty much the same gender lines. There would, as a concession to existing mainstream designations, perhaps be a smattering of men and women of color and white women secreted away in a few executive positions.

It's doubtful that Marjorie would have employed only women, provided child care, self-protection courses, profit sharing, investment groups and generous retirement plans for her employees. Neither would she have played Tori, Nina Simone, Me'Shell, Shonen Knife, Sinéad and Yma Sumac over the factory loudspeakers to boost morale, meanwhile revolutionizing the advertising industry's image of women and children with her sheer buying power.

Good businesswomen just don't take risks like that.

So let's, shall we, define risk:

A maneuver which has neither a past nor a guaranteeable future generating profits is a risk.

It's a risk for women to run the show because the show was designed to be run by an elite group of white men.

Women will never be an elite group of white men, so the show was not designed to be run by us.

Deedle dee doo, Catch-22.

When I feel defeated or frustrated or just dang upset because
there is simply no sidestepping this shitty reality, I sometimes
call my sister. She says, "Count your blessings, ya' lucky hooker.
Don't be bitter. Your face gets all ugly when you're bitter."

I represent maybe .0001 percent of cuntlovin' ladies
throughout history who have been and continue to be bored to
death with the plights of this reality.

Sometimes though, I *feel* like being bitter because I wake up
in the morning and just have to face the fact that within this
economic model, *it makes perfect sense* for Kevin Costner to
spend more money on a single, fully lunkheaded movie that
contributes absolutely nothing to society than the entire nation
of El Salvador sees in one year.

My face gets all ugly and I call my sister and she reminds me
I'm a lucky hooker when I think about the multitudes of women
who are creating desperately needed and appreciated products
that have no *physical place* within the capitalist, patriarchal
economic model and—like women artists—struggle to prove our
existence long before advancing upon the struggle to *survive*.

I work with a woman named Kathleen Gasperini who publishes
W.I.G. (Women in General) magazine. *W.I.G.* is focused on
giving women a place to write about our fabulous lives and
adventures living them, the music and sports that move us, our
poetry and stories, interviews with other women living their
fabulous lives and our battles with cancer, violence, poverty,
racial and sexual hatred, drugs and/or eating disorders.

Ms. Gasperini has a difficult time finding investors because her magazine does not reflect standard "women's interests" found in other culturally accepted "women's magazines."

Here is what potential investors say to Ms. Gasperini, "There's no section for your magazine in the stores. It can't be in the sports section. It's not just about fitness and health. Neither is it for new mothers, brides-to-be, lesbians or feminists. If you focused more on fashion and make-up, we'd be happy to invest because then we'd know how to market it and people would know where to find it."

The fact that *W.I.G.* is one of a handful of like-minded, brilliant magazines—*Bitch, Bust* and *Hues* come readily to mind—doesn't seem to inspire any thoughts about a market of consumers who represent an acute demand for what these magazines supply.

Once upon a time, Kathleen Gasperini spent two months begging her printers to be patient for the money she owed them, as a gentleman who runs a major magazine publishing company had expressed an interest in investing in *W.I.G.* Week after week they played phone tag, Kathleen's heart lodged in her throat.

When she finally met with him, he had the following nugget of inspiration to impart:

"You are the wrong gender for what we are focusing on at this time. The market is going crazy for young men right now."

Circulation for the first issue of *W.I.G.* was five thousand.

Circulation for *W.I.G.*'s fourth issue was fifty thousand.

For a market that does not exist, fifty thousand consumers is a pretty heady figure, considering *W.I.G.* sales are dependent upon word of mouth in lieu of national advertising and promotion. Stores do not have a section for magazines such as *W.I.G.* because it is by, for and about women, on our terms.

Our culture does not provide a place for that.

There is—*literally*—no place for products of this kind.

A small amount of research in American history illuminates how just about every "right" and "freedom" people of color and white women achieved was the result of economics. The Civil War was not about compassion and decency, it was about real estate. The alleged "rights" of "land settlements bestowed" upon Native tribes are also real estate. Granting white women and people of color the "right" to vote was about creating a class of peon workers who were less able to grumble over the poor pay and working conditions when they had such a glorious "right" as casting ballots that placed a variety of white men in office.

Hoop dee doo.

In our society's time-tested economic model, men make and women consume. Our fingernail polishes, snowboards, vacuum cleaners, computers, clothes—pretty much most of our stuff— was manufactured by male-dominated and -owned companies. Utilities and credit card companies claim yet another portion of our income for the male producers that make stuff for us ladies.

Accordingly, one of our most promising stakes of power is our indisputed role as consumers.

As consumers, we exist.

This is a resource that is presently part of our reality.

Exploit the fuck out of it.

Cuntlovin' Consumerism

Time and money are power.

Conscious decision-making about the expenditure of both nourishes a market that is somehow considered "fledgling," although it represents 51 percent of the population.

Many phallocentric religious organizations, from the Promise Keepers to the Church of Latter Day Saints heartily extol the benefits of keeping money in the community of the brethren.

Patriarchal society never has to bother preaching the benefits of keeping the money with the men because, at present, there's no place else for it to go.

In the marketplace of the patriarchy, the "competition" tends to be people living in Mexican, Latin American, South African and Southeast Asian communities (often referred to as "guerrilla terrorists"), fighting for the right to live on the planet with an identity other than that of expendable factory worker-slaves.

It sounds *terribly* ideological to say women's power as consumers is a major economic stronghold, but it seems the most promising strategy that does not involve retreat.

Cuntlovin' Consumerism is a matter of research and potential inconvenience.

It requires no thought to amble to the Mega Food-O-Rama and buy a name-brand loaf of bread. Finding a bakery in your community that is owned by a woman struggling to bring up three children by herself may take a bit of phone work. Because this baker does not produce and distribute on the massive scale of Wonder Bread, her product will be of higher quality and nutritional value, but it may also be more expensive.

Cuntlovin' Consumerism is a matter of common sense.

When it becomes the custom to visit only women gynecologists, naturopaths and midwives, the clientele of male
doctors will fluctuate precariously, and cuntcare will eventually become the sole women-dominated field in the medical
industry outside nursing.

Cuntlovin' Consumerism is a matter of commitment.

The only women-owned bookstore you know of is twenty-
five miles away from your house. Once a month, you and your
friends make a special trip to this store instead of bopping into
the local Mega-Book-O-Rama whenever you happen upon
disposable income.

Try this experimental test.

You will need a sheet of gold stars to conduct it properly.

Stand in the middle of your kitchen. Scan every single
appliance, work of art, food product, fixture and piece of furniture
in the room. Place everything in one of three categories:

1. Definitely/probably produced by women or a woman-
    run corporation.
2. You aren't sure.
3. Definitely/probably produced by men or a male-run
    corporation.

Every time your vision rests upon something that falls into
category #1, put a gold star on it. After you have perused the
contents of every cupboard and drawer, count up the number of
gold stars.

Unless you have already researched the matter and actively

c
u
n
t

sought out products made by women, your kitchen will not be very golden starry.

Conduct this experiment in every room of your house.

Now, live your life from this day forward with the objective of filling your home with as many gold stars as possible.

The day you got gold stars on most all of your stuff will be the last day of the patriarchal age as far you, the consumer, are concerned.

Cuntlovin' Investment Portfolio

An investment is a portion of capital (money or time) that is spent now for bigger, better results later.

There are a number of different kinds of investments.

One is the personal investment. This is where you buy a coffee maker that you set before you go to bed, so that in the morning, you will have time to do yoga, which in turn, centers you for the day ahead and subsequently helps you make optimal decisions that improve the quality of your life day by day.

Another investment is the pain-in-the-ass-job investment. This is where you sacrifice X amount of time each and every week Whoring yourself at some meaningless job in order to finance your life so you can, say, finish your book.

Yet another kind of investment, the kind we're concerned with here, is a group investment. This involves getting your women friends or family members together and figuring out how much capital you have, collectively, to invest.

First you determine how much time you have to invest in your investment group.

Then you figure out money and resources.

If each of you has five dollars, and there are ten of you, that is fifty dollars. *The amount of money you have is not important.* What *is* important is how you answer the following question:

How can we make this fifty dollars into one hundred dollars?

This is the beginning of a Cuntlovin' Investment Portfolio.

The best way to have a productive investment group is to exploit the resources you already have available to you, rather than expending energy looking for the resources you imagine are necessary. I'm gonna say this again in a few moments because it's a fundamental rule here.

Perhaps two women in your group are seamstresses, one has an industrial sewing machine in her closet, another inherited a garage full of fabric from her great-grandmother, you happen to be a genius at computer design and the remaining three are very talented songwriters and musicians.

Hmmmm.

Seems like the eight of you should be able to bring all those things together in a lucrative manner.

How?

I haven't the faintest clue.

That is where the brilliance of your investment group comes in.

An investment group meets on a regular basis and focuses energy on the process of making collective capital experience gains.

Your group may decide to start a business, play the women-owned companies that have gone public on the stock market, present an investment proposal to your local woman-run record company, have bake sales or throw huge, elaborately themed parties where you charge people to get in.

Once again, I underscore the following: The challenge for an investment group is exploiting the resources you have readily available. This yields *much better results* than agonizing over how to make something out of a good, but presently inaccessible idea.

When an investment group gets enough capital, it pays dividends to the group's members, which helps improve the quality of life; it re-invests or loans money to woman-run businesses or production companies; it starts a scholarship fund or buys an entire city block to provide housing to young women athletes, scholars and artists who are fighting like the devil to survive and fulfill dreams at the same time.

Time and money are power.

When women pro-actively seize both, we take power.

Every iota of power women claim and use to the advantage of our sisters brings the destructive patriarchal age that much closer to its timely, timely, timely end.

It has been a long time, but the Goddess is waking up from her nap.

She's yawning, stretching her muscles and scratching her big beautiful butt. Rest assured, the Goddess has a thing or two to say about man as the maker. When the Goddess gets the sleep out of her eyes, I daresay my face won't have many opportunities to get all ugly about cultural atrocities like Kevin Costner movies.

But my sister will probably always remind me I'm a lucky
hooker.

P.S.
You're a Big Cunt now.
You find out who Mammon is.

reconciliation

Who the Old Woman with Black Eyeballs that Swallow You in Love Is

the end

The end of this book came to me in a message from an old woman in a dream. What follows is a verbatim account of this dream, written in my journal directly after waking up.

In Dream that woke me up.

I am a thirteen-or-so-year-old Latino boy. I am freaking out in some room that feels like a place where the community gathers, but it's not a church. I—the young boy—am angry beyond orange, beyond red, beyond white. People are futilely trying to physically restrain me. Some white men have served an unnamed injustice to my people. *Mi familia.* I want to kill. I want their blood to stain my hands. I want to pull their hearts from their chests. No one can control me.

An old woman walks into the room. All attention falls upon her. I feel her black eyes bore into my being, but still, I thrash and fight to get to the white men, outside the place where I am.

The old woman walks directly up to me. She takes my wrists in her hands, and my strength—which has defied every woman, child and man in the room—is useless against her.

Holding my wrists, she gently brings my arms down to my sides and begins to cry, oh, she cries from the depths of every soul that has ever graced this planet.

Through her tears, she calmly, soothingly whispers, "Don't you know, don't you know, only our stories can fight against these men. Only our words. You must say, 'Excuse me, sir, but I would like to tell you this story about my grandmother.' And the man will listen, our words will enter his heart, and kill his power from the inside."

She stares into me.

"Only our stories. Only our words."

She continues crying as she says all this, she is crying for ancestors, for grandchildren, for all the civilizations which have been decimated.

Her crying is in my body.

My sleeping, dreaming body.

Her crying storms through the core of my heart. Her crying, *the feeling*, not the sound, her crying wakes me up.

There are no tears on my face.

Her crying is inside me.

This is the message from the old woman with black eyeballs that swallow you in love and make you understand there is nothing to fear.

Blessed Be.
Grandmother.
Cunt.

Cuntlovin' Guide to the Universe

There's only one way to create a cuntlovin' universe: Get off the ol' tush and make it happen. As the beloved and highly esteemed Ali Ø. never lets me forget: "Baby, you don't get what you deserve, you get what you negotiate."

The 1998 September/October issue of the *Utne Reader* features an article about two young women who personify some of the more crucial aspects of negotiating a cuntlovin' universe.

The Fabulous Misses Julia Steinmetz and Jessica Peterson—twenty-one-year-old students attending Carleton College in Northfield, Minnesota—are negotiating something of a fashion/genderfuck empire. The GLAM Dyke Rescue Unit is their personal response to pop culture, fashion, gender roles and social revolution. By the simple initial act of writing a manifesto, the Fabulous Misses have formulated their very own platform. They sell their manifesto for a dollar, and have developed very reasonably priced mail-order GLAM kits for people who may need a little help getting glamorous.

Both GLAM and the Fabulous Misses are very inspiring because they know in their hearts that they have absolutely inalienable rights to:

1. Critically examine social norms.
2. Develop their own system of beliefs.
3. Brilliantly co-opt that which is in accord with those beliefs.

4. Ruthlessly chuck that which is in discord with those beliefs.

5. Make manifest applicable exemplifications of their beliefs.

6. Earn money educating people about their beliefs.

7. Have a good-assed time doin' it.

The projects, concerns and individuals included in this listing reflect examples of the round, womanly, ass-busting efforts that are required when one is committed to negotiating a universe that revolves around the power of women. Many—not all, but many—of the women in this listing must maintain gainful employment concurrent to, say, publishing a magazine or shooting a feature-length film. Some of the women who coordinate these two realities also support, raise and love a kid, or four.

It's impossible to create an *exhaustive* Cuntlovin' Guide to the Universe because there are so many awesome people who are brilliant and shining. What I have compiled for you is meant to be the seed of a much larger database you create, sustain and consistently utilize for yourself. I have included filmmakers, web resources, magazines and businesses/ organizations that in some way or another challenge the existence of cunthatred in our society by being fighting and strong and wicked badass.

This resource guide was created with the assistance of Lisa Jervis (read her magazine), Holly Morris (watch her documentary series), Harper Carter (watch her films), Kathleen Gasperini (read her magazine), Panacea Theriac (see her puppet show), the women at Seal Press (buy their books), Allison Wolfe (listen to her music) and Sadie Shaw (watch her films).

Magazines

The deal with most of these magazines is they have just enough (and sometimes not quite that much) money to keep publishing. Every time you hold one of these magazines in your hot little hands, *know this:* A group of women experienced grueling hours and incessant heart palpitations in order to come up with the funding to deliver this product to you. Pretty much all of the information in this listing is regularly featured in these magazines. The following magazines represent the meat and potatoes for accessing cuntlovin' resources.

Bitch, 3128 16th Street, Box 201, San Francisco, CA 94103, ljervis@sirius.com. "Feminist response to pop culture." Scathing appraisals of cunthatred in our culture, articles and interviews that take on many sides of an issue. All by itself, *Bitch* is an *unbelievable* fount of resources. The phone company refused to list this riveting-assed mag's number for a long time, but in the end *Bitch* triumphed. I have not listed their number. In the spirit of issuing a big "fuck you" to large corporations that have no room for cuntlove, please call (415) 555-1212 and ask the operator for *Bitch's* phone number.

Bust, P.O. Box 319, Ansonia Station, New York, NY 10023, www.bust.com. Super cool, super cool, super cool!!! Great read for dykes, bi-ladies, straight chicks and boys! Interviews, comix, essays. Informative, hilarious and serious all at the same time.

Themed issues explore various topics of interest to women who think and laugh.

conmoción: revista y red revolucionaria de lesbianas latinas, 1521 Alton Road #336, Miami Beach, FL 33139, (305) 751-8385. In glorious Español y Inglés. Awesome magazine! Photos, essays, erotica. Sexy, sexy mag that's beautifully designed. The writing is consistently mesmerizing, compelling and a damn turn-on.

Fat Girl: A Zine for Fat Dykes and the Women Who Want Them, 2215-R Market St. #197, San Francisco, CA 94114, (415) 522-8733, selene@sirius.com. Very erotic, awesome writing, super inspiring. This gorgeous magazine is for anyone who has ever experienced alienation because of the perception of body image in our culture, whether you weigh in at three hundred or eighty-five pounds.

Girljock, Rox-A-Tronic Publishing, P.O. Box 882723, San Francisco, CA 94188-2723, www.tezcat.com/ ~ksbrooks/Gj/gjnew. The first women's sports magazine to grace the planet in a cuntlovin' way. *Girljock* rocks. Besides all the killer sports stuff, interviews and music reviews, they have charming articles like, "How to Be Fearless" and "How to Be Friendly." Lighthearted, humorous and take no prisoners to the core.

Hip Mama, P.O. Box 9097, Oakland, CA 94613, www.hipmama.com. *The most important* magazine in the whole wide world. *Hip Mama* is supposed to pertain to, well, hip mamas, but I'm not even planning *to plan* to have kids and I voraciously consume each issue. *Hip Mama* always has these articles that I end up clipping out and keeping in my backpack to read over and over again when I'm on the bus. As of this writing, I've read "Mom's Just Want to Get Paid" at least twenty-eight times. No lie. Published by a single mother who is a total genius. Subscribe.

HUES (Hear Us Emerging Sisters), P.O. Box 3620, Duluth, MN 55803-3620, (218) 728-5507, www.hues.net. As of this writing, *HUES* is the Cinderella of the cuntlovin' magazine universe. New Moon Publishing (which also publishes *New Moon· the Magazine for Girls and Their Dreams*) has made it possible for *HUES* to increase their frequency rate from two times a year to bimonthly. This represents the first time an *awesome, fully cuntlovin' magazine* has received major funding. When yer' done ogling all the back issues you may have missed, read *HUES* founder Ophira Edut's new anthology, *Adiós, Barbie: Young Women Write About Body Image and Identity.*

W.I.G. (Women In General), P.O. Box 158, Heber City, UT 84032, (801) 654-5398, www.wigmag.com. A winsome combination of sports, culture, interviews and discussion of issues pertinent to women, *W.I.G.* is a general magazine for women. It used to be quarterly, but had to scale down to publishing two print issues a year, with an online version that is updated bimonthly. *W.I.G.* founded Boarding for Breast Cancer, which has become one of the biggest fundraising events for breast cancer research in the country.

If you haven't checked out *Mode* or *Jump,* you probably should. They are more or less mainstream glossy mags with "luxuries" like a budget and paid employees. Both, however, represent a victory for cuntlovin' women because they give us a different, healthier, fully unapologetic way of looking at our bodies.

Websites

If you are unfamiliar with the web, read *SurferGrrrls* by Laurel Gilbert and Crystal Kile and/or *Net Chick* by Carla Sinclair. Both of these books are comprehensive, nonintimidating and quintessentially cuntlovin'.

My guiding principle for surfing the web is:
    Where there's ladies, there's links.
My favorite hubs of activity at present are:
www.heck.com/annie/annieabout
www.estronet.com
www.gurl.com
www.webgrrrl.com
www.wench.com
www.adventuredivas.com
www.yin.org
www.michfest.com
Why, there's even a website related to this book:
www.kalikunti.com

My Thirteen Favorite Cuntlovin' Movies of All Time
Entertainment and advertising executives are very fond of the argument that negativity does not spawn negativity. This is bad math. "We do not affect society's actions," they say. "We just

want everyone to have a good time at the flicks."

And I am very fond of the argument that physical images in the material world affect each individual in the exact same manner as dream images in the unconscious world. I do not know why we consciously interpret our dreams but rarely take the trouble to consciously interpret our waking hours. There really is no difference between being awake and being asleep. Images and situations are consistently presented, and whether or not you're aware of it, you internalize, process or deny everything, however your heart, brain and history dictates.

And so, believing this has made me very aware of the importance of counter-attacking negative images with positive ones. I *need* to see images of women being violent towards men because these are the images that 100 percent counter all the images of violence and objectification directed towards women that I see in my society almost every day.

I cannot adequately describe the intense blaze of deeply rooted vindication that exploded in my body when Louise killed the dude who was about to rape Thelma in the parking lot of a honky tonk bar. I whooped in the theater. That scene represented *the first time in my life* I sat in a crowded room with hundreds of Americans, collectively witnessing a woman reach critical mass and respond accordingly. A memory of sexual assault lurked in Louise's mind. Every fiber of her being rebelled at the notion of her dear friend sharing such a memory. So, ol' Louise, she put a stop to it. Blew away the piece of shit who was presenting Thelma with this potential memory.

La Femme Nikita

The unparalleled and much-emulated classic. A very violent film about a woman trained intensely for years to eventually become a calculated killing machine. Worth watching many times over.

Gloria

Gena Rowlands kills mafia men while saving the life of a six-year-old kid who says stuff like, "I'm the man, Gloria. You're not the man. *I'm the man.*" Gloria chain-smokes, is the definition of negotiation, has lotsa money, maintains serious connections with the underworld and is an ardent slave to fashion.

Born in Flames

A cult classic, kinda sci-fi-ish and set in a postapocalyptic future. I consider this film a rite of passage for every woman in America. Directed by the chronically effulgent Ms. Lizzy Borden.

The Long Kiss Goodnight

Geena Davis kills men. Her overbite shines like god. Samuel L. Jackson helps her. Every time I see this movie, I wish they were my parents.

Set It Off

Five women get fed up with the lame-assed injustices in this world and start robbing banks. For a long time, I avoided this flick because I knew the ladies don't get to ride off into the sunset. Yes, this is crushing, but it's a beautiful movie. Queen Latifah is sexier than Julio Iglesias in his prime.

Freeway

Reese Witherspoon plays Little Red Riding Hood. Watching her maul Keifer Sutherland improved the quality of my life because I can't stand to look at his loathsome face in any context. And boy, is his face loathsome by the time ol' Reese is done with him. The casting is superb. Brooke Sheilds plays Keifer's equally loathsome wife and Amanda Plummer's brief performance as Reese's crack-addict Whore mom is positively breathtaking.

I Shot Andy Warhol

Lily Taylor plays Valerie Solanas, author of the *S.C.U.M.* (Society for Cutting Up Men) *Manifesto*. Valerie Solanas shot Andy Warhol because he was a pompous asshole. I like this movie because I like Valerie Solanas (and Lily Taylor!), and I like Valerie Solanas because she represents an extreme hatred of men. When balanced with the relatively extreme passivity women are generally portrayed with, the result is generally a very nice lady who don't take no shit. To create and sustain this balance, I believe, women must have the opportunity to experience both extremes. For optimal enjoyment, read the *S.C.U.M. Manifesto* before watching this movie.

Pippi Longstocking series

Don't watch Pippi's movies because you are too lazy to read her books. Watch Pippi's movies because you already read all her books and it's raining outside and you are depressed and a ray of light shines in your mind and you realize: You need Pippi. Pippi doesn't kill men. She's generally content just throwing them in trees.

251

Thelma and Louise

Geena Davis and that damn winsome smile of hers again. This time she and Susan Sarandon kill men. Geena fucks Brad Pitt (back when Brad still had a soul). Thelma and Louise literally ride off a cliff into the sunset, which is as heartbreaking as when nobody ran off into the sunset in *Set It Off.* How come ladies never seem to get away?

The Watermelon Woman

One of my few favorite movies that doesn't feature men being killed by women. Cheryl Dunye wrote, directed and stars in this *beyond* compelling and beautiful film. It's a documentary about searching for this gorgeous actress from the 1930s, known only as "The Watermelon Woman." But the creation of the documentary is symbolic of what the filmmaker is going through in her personal life as she makes the film. A mirror in a mirror, shining blinding point-blank and pretty as can be at the same time.

I've Heard the Mermaids Singing

The cutest movie! So cute! About this girl named Polly who will be the dork of your heart within the first ten minutes of the film! No men get killed in this one either but who cares when the protagonist is so dang darling.

Butterfly Kiss

Amanda Plummer plays a psycho killer. She kills pretty much indiscriminately. I love this movie because a.) Amanda Plummer is a freckin' genius and b.) it has *the best ending I have ever seen in my life,* which unfortunately, does not entail anyone riding off into any sunset, either.

The Bandit Queen

This movie will upset you. It is very upsetting. Based on the life of Phoolan Devi, India's famed Bandit Queen. Since some important background information cannot be communicated through the medium of film, I strongly recommend reading *The Bandit Queen,* by Mala Sen, before watching the movie. Every time I see this film with friends, we hafta pause it for me to explain circumstances that I learned from reading the book. Regardless, it is a beautiful, beautiful story and should not be missed. After the film was made, Phoolan Devi was released from prison and went on to be voted a Member of Parliament. This vindicates matters most deliciously; however, as of this writing, Ms. Devi is under house arrest in her home state of Uttar Pradesh.

Filmmakers

Women have been making movies for a long time. Men have been running the companies that distribute movies on a mass scale across the world for a long time. Generally, women don't make movies men feel compelled to distribute. This creates the illusion that women don't make movies.

Film Fatales: Independent Women Directors is a book that dispels this illusion. Featuring biographical essays and filmographies of thirty-three filmmakers who have collectively produced over two hundred and twenty films, *Film Fatales* is a cornerstone resource for any cuntlovin' film library. Nine distribution companies that deliver these films to your door are listed at the back of the book. By contacting any of these film distribution companies and pooling resources with your friends, you can find out how to have your own private film festival, thus bypassing all of the illusions our culture presents to us.

Order catalogs from the following distribution companies, and be on the lookout for the awe-inspiring independent filmmakers who follow.

Video Data Bank, School of the Art Institute of Chicago, 375 Wabash Avenue, Chicago, IL 60603, (312) 345-3550.

Women Make Movies, 462 Broadway, Suite 500D, New York, NY 10013, (212) 925-0606.

CFDC, 37 Hannah Avenue, Toronto, Ontario, M6H1W8, Canada, (416) 588-0725, cfmdc@interlog.com.

Zeitgeist Films, 247 Centre Street, Second Floor, New York, NY 10013, (212) 274-1989, mail@zeitgeistfilm.com.

First Run Features, 153 Waverly Place, New York, NY 10014, (212) 243-0600.

Third World Newsreel, 335 W. 38th Street, Fifth Floor, New York, NY 10018, (212) 947-9277.

Frameline, 346 9th Street, San Francisco, CA 94103, (415) 703-8650.

Jamika Ajalon

Tula Asselanis

Sadie Benning

Lana Bernberg

Julianna Berg

Lizzie Borden

Harper Carter

Christian Cegavske

Robin Cline

Cheryl Dunye

Katrina Flener

Michelle Handelmann

Bridget Irish

Sarah Jacobson

Saskia Jell

Miranda July (Miranda July is building an empire. She's got this "Big Miss Moviola [video] Chainletter" thing going on that you can contribute to as well as purchase. Freckin' genius.) Contact Big Miss Moviola, P.O. Box 14284, Portland, OR 97293.

Ruth Leitman

Kate McCabe

Lisa Ann Nordstrom

Jennifer Reeder

Vanessa Renwick

Jeri Cain Rossi

Machiko Salto

Sadie Shaw

c
u
n
t
l
o
v
i
n'

g
u
i
d
e

Cuntlovin' Record Companies

The vast majority of people creating beautiful cuntlovin' music do not get airtime on the MTeeVee. Supporting cuntlovin' musicians, like independent filmmakers, often involves requesting catalogs from small record companies. Here are a few:

Chainsaw Records
P.O. Box 1151, Olympia, WA 98507, www.chainsaw.com

Kill Rock Stars
Slim Moon owns Kill Rocks Stars and he's a boy. But ninety percent of the people he employs are women and most of the records they release are by women. 120 NE State Street #418, Olympia, WA 98501, (360) 357-9732

Righteous Babe Records
P.O. Box 95, Ellicott Station, Buffalo, NY 14205, (716) 852-8020 phone, (716) 852-2741 fax

Simba Music
2842 Adeline Street, Suite 2, Oakland, CA 94608, (510) 763-6670, simbamusic@sprynet.com

Villa VillaKula Records
P.O. Box 1929, Boston, MA 02205

Win Records
P.O. Box 26811, Los Angeles, CA 90026-0811
www.winrecords.com

Bookstores and Publishing Companies

Recently, I was bummin' harder than wrought iron. My mother, sister, all my friends, three days of highly stimulating debauchery and a goddamn manicure could not put Humpty together again. Mired in misery, I unsuspectingly read Dolly Parton's autobiography, *My Life and Other Unfinished Business*. Ms. Parton's words held the magic incantation to pick me up, dust me off and send me on my ecstatic way. This is not the first time a book has saved my sorry ass and it damn straight won't be the last.

Books are powerful. Books have been the cornerstone of cuntlovin' communication since language evolved into the written word. Even more powerful is the fact that many, many brilliant books are written by cuntlovin' women who do not have the economic draw of ultra-mega stars like Dolly Parton. Meanwhile, many relatively small companies have been publishing and selling books for decades.

Purchasing books from women-owned bookstores is one of the most important things a cuntlovin' consumer can do. In bookstores owned by large corporations, one must look for books by, for and about women. This is inherently not the case in women-owned bookstores, which often double as cultural hubs for the communities they serve.

If you want to know how to change the oil filter in your car, a women-owned bookstore will carry car repair manuals that *assume* women are interested in maintaining their equipment. A seemingly minor distinction, perhaps, but one that also makes all the difference in the whole wide world.

Feminist Bookstore News has created an entire network of women-owned bookstores all across the country—and they've compiled a list. Send for the list (free) or a sample of their magazine ($6). Contact them at: P.O. Box 882554, San Francisco, CA 94188, (415) 642-9993. Or get online and check out their website at www.FemBookNet.com.

All women-run publishing companies have catalogs and/or websites featuring veritably thousands of titles of pertinent interest to cuntlovin' women. Obviously, there is the incomparable Seal Press, publisher of this book. Their web address is www.sealpress.com. Many publishing companies provide links to other companies. To get started on a nice little web surf, check out: www.firebrandbooks.com; www.spinsters-ink.com; www.pressgang.bc.ca.

Always bop to a neighborhood women-owned bookstore or get online and explore these sights before bopping down to the local Mega-O-Rama Book Emporium in your community.

Sex Stores Galore!!!!
Read "Orgasms From Cunts" again if you don't remember how and why these establishments are so very important.

Good Vibrations
938 Howard Street #101, San Francisco, CA 94103, (800) 289-8423.

Toys in Babeland
707 E. Pike Street, Seattle, WA 91822, (800) 658-9119
54 Rivington Street, New York, NY 10002, www.babeland.com

It's My Pleasure
4258 SE Hawthorne Boulevard, Portland, OR 97215, (503) 236-0505.

A Woman's Touch
600 Williamson Street, Madison, WI 53703, (888) 621-8880,
www.a-womans-touch.com.

Grand Opening
318 Harvard Street, Suite 32, The Arcade Building, Brookline,
MA 02146, (617) 312-2626.

Eve's Garden
119 W. 57th Street, Suite 420, New York, NY 10019-2383,
(800) 848-3837.

Misc. Cuntlovin' Enterprises

The Michigan Womyn's Music Festival, WWTMC, P.O. Box 22,
Walhalla, MI 49458, (610) 767-4766, www.michfest.com. You
hafta go to this festival at least one time in your life. You
positively hafta see what women create out there in the Michigan
boondocks. Moslem people often judge their lives by the criteria
of whether or not they have been to Mecca. And so it is with
Michigan if you're a cuntlovin' lady.

Each year's handbook is also, by itself, an extraordinary
resource guide. It lists how to get in touch with every musician,
businesswoman, filmmaker, publication and workshop pre-
senter involved with that year's festival.

Maat Dompin, Auto Road, Auto, WV, 24917, (304) 497-3737.
I heard about this project at the Michigan Womyn's Festival. Maat
Dompin is a group of women working to create an entire commu-
nity for women of color. They sell T-shirts and stuff, too.

Free Speech TV, (303) 442-5693, fstv@fstv.org, www.freespeech.com. As fate had it, I happened upon this television station by absolute accident. FSTV airs films by independent women filmmakers, as well as compelling documentaries on subjects even public television shys away from. From "Dyke TV" and "Mumia Abu Jamal: On Death Row" to "Fresh Talk: Youth and Sexuality," FSTV is the first out 'n out socially responsible television station I have ever seen. Contact them to find out what channel FSTV airs on in your area.

GLAM Dyke Rescue Unit, Box 385, Northfield, MN 55057. See intro to this guide. GLAM Manifestoes are available for a dollar. They also sell three mail-order kits: The $5 GLAM Primer, contains "everyday performance activities for the beginner," the $20 GLAM Revolutionary Beginner's Campaign Kit includes sunglasses, lipsticks and toy handcuffs and the $35 Advanced GLAM Kit is resplendent with a made-to-order miniskirt, feather boa and other accessories.

Ladies Art Revival, P.O. Box 217, Morristown, NJ 08057, ladiesartrevival@hotmail.com. Film and zine distribution company. They also sell panties that say, "I (heart) My Cunt."

One Angry Girl, P.O. Box 674, North Cambridge, MA 02141, (888) ANGRY-11, www.ici.net/cust_pages/angrygrl/angrygrl. T-shirts with slogans like, "Fuck Your Fascist Beauty Standards" and "Well-Behaved Women Rarely Make History."

Blood Sisters Québec Concordia, Qpirg room 101, 2130 rue
Mackay, Montréal, Québec, H3G 2J1 Canada, (514) 848-7585,
bloodsisters@cug.concordia.ca. (See the "Blood and Cunts"
chapter for the lowdown on Bloodsisters.)

Lisa Buttonow, P.O. Box 1245, Madison, WI 53701-1245,
(608) 258-1681. She makes cunt soap!! Beautiful handmade
cunt soaps for getting' clean 'n shiny in the shower! Hee-Haw.

Sticker Sisters, P.O. Box 11480, Takoma Park, MD 20913,
www.stickersisters.com. A sticker company started by a high-
school girl named Ariel Fox. Sticker Sisters is all about creating
positive messages for [young] women. This is reason enough to
send for a catalog, but Ms. Fox might also have some advice for
other young girls who want to start their own companies. Send
two stamps and you'll receive a catalog in the mail.

About-Face, P.O. Box 77665, San Francisco, CA 94107,
(415) 436-0212, www.about-face.org. Founder Kathy Bruin and
comrades traipse through the streets of San Francisco, wheat-
pasting posters of emaciated models with the slogan "Stop
Starvation Imagery." Someone in every American city should
take it upon themselves to poetically attack cunthatred.

A Brain Exercise
Lots of people surf the web, but few know the concept of surfing
the library. Library surfing is a brain workout that opens your
mind to influences outside your normal realm of consciousness.
A good day's library surf is a total head rush, mindfuck freakout.

I *highly* recommend it.

In order to surf the library, one must set aside as much time as humanly possible. *Absolutely no less* than four hours. Enter the library with the agenda of a newborn lamb. Spin around three times, walk in a direction, find a shelf, pick a book and read it for a while. Then move on, never paying attention to where you are going or what book your hand rests on. Pull books off the shelf indiscriminately. Open to a page and start reading. You must read at least two pages before moving on. You'll find truly riveting material that might lay claim to your passions, but don't let any book suck you in for too long. Keep movin'.

When you force yourself to investigate stuff you've never, ever thought about before, you open up.

I have risked my life to save a fucken *pigeon* on a freeway offramp. I love animals with all my heart. Always have. Can't eat 'em. Love 'em, love 'em, respect 'em, love 'em. It was on a library surf, however, that I developed an appreciation for taxidermy. It is a painstakingly precise art form. Taxidermy requires patience, an ornate attention to detail, many intricate processes and mind-boggling amounts of time. Taxidermy came into my life while I was writing this book. I was very surprised and perversely enchanted to learn I had so much in common with a taxidermist. I figure if, on a single library surf, I can learn to respect something so far afield from what I perceive to be a deeply ingrained love for all life forms, then something very powerful is in the ol' midst.

Have a nice, cuntlovin' day now, ya hear.

Selected Bibliography and Reading List

Acker, Kathy. *In Memoriam to Identity.* New York: Pantheon, 1992.

Acker, Kathy. *Blood and Guts in High School.* New York: Grover Weidenfeld, 1989.

Allen, Paula Gunn. *Spiderwoman's Granddaughters.* Boston: Beacon, 1989.

Allison, Dorothy. *Bastard Out of Carolina.* New York: Dutton, 1992.

Allison, Dorothy. *Two or Three Things I Know for Sure.* New York: Dutton, 1995.

Alsop, Gulielma Fell, M.D. and McBride, Mary F. *Arms and the Girl: A Guide to Personal Adjustment in War Work and War Marriage.* City: Press, 1943.

Angelou, Maya. *I Know Why the Caged Bird Sings.* New York: Random House, 1970.

Angelou, Maya. *Just Give Me a Cool Drink of Water 'Fore I Die: The Poetry of Maya Angelou.* New York: Random House, 1971.

Atwood, Margaret. *The Handmaid's Tale.* Boston: G. K. Hall, 1987.

Block, Francesca Lia. *Weetzie Bat.* New York: Harper & Row, 1989.

Block, Francesca Lia. *Girl Goddess #9.* New York: HarperCollins, 1996.

Brown, Judith C. *Immodest Acts: The Life of a Lesbian Nun in Renaissance Italy.* New York: Oxford University Press, 1986.

Brownmiller, Susan. *Against Our Will: Men, Women and Rape.* New York: Simon & Schuster, 1975.

Bufwack, Mary A. *Finding Her Voice: The Saga of Women in Country Music.* New York: Crown, 1993.

Burgos-Debray, Elisabeth, ed. *I, Rigoberta Menchú: An Indian Woman in Guatemala.* London, U.K: Verso, 1984.

Cameron, Anne. *Daughters of Copper Woman*. Vancouver B.C:
Press Gang, 1981.

Caprio, Frank S., M.D. *Female Homosexuality: A Psychodynamic
Study of Lesbianism*. New York: Citadel, 1954.

Carter, Angela. *The Bloody Chamber and Other Stories*. New York:
Harper & Row, 1979

Carter, Angela. *The Old Wives' Fairy Tale Book*. New York:
Pantheon, 1995.

Castillo, Ana. *The Mixquiahuala Letters*. Binghampton, N.Y:
Bilingual Press, 1986.

Ceronetti, Guido. *The Silence of the Body: Materials For the Study
of Medicine*. New York: Farrar, Straus & Giroux, Year

Chicago, Judy. *Beyond the Flower: The Autobiography of a
Feminist Artist*. New York: Viking, 1996.

Cohen, David, ed. *The Circle of Life: Rituals from the Human
Family Album*. New York: Harper, 1991.

Crawford, Joan. *My Way of Life*. New York: Pocket Books, 1972.

Dunn, Katherine. *Geek Love*. New York: Warner, 1983.

Dunn, Katherine. *Attic*. New York: Warner, 1990.

Eisler, Riane T. *The Chalice and The Blade: Our History, Our
Future*. Cambridge, MA: Harper & Row, 1987.

Eisler, Riane T. *Sacred Pleasure: Sex, Myth and the Politics of the
Body*. San Francisco: Harper San Francisco, 1995.

El Saadawi, Nawal. *Woman at Point Zero*. City: Zed Books, 1984.

Ellison, Katherine W. *Imelda: Steel Butterfly of the Philippines*.
New York: McGraw-Hill, 1988.

Erdrich, Louise. *Love Medicine*. New York: Holt, Reinhart & Winston, 1984.

Erdrich, Louise. *Tracks.* Boston: G. K. Hall, 1989.

Findlen, Barbara, ed. *Listen Up: Voices from the Next Feminist Generation.* Seattle: Seal, 1995.

French, Marilyn. *Beyond Power: On Women, Men, and Morals.* New York: Summit, 1985.

French, Marilyn. *The War Against Women.* New York: Summit, 1992.

Galeano, Eduardo. *Memory of Fire* (a trilogy): *Genesis, Faces and Masks, Century of the Wind.* New York: Pantheon, 1985.

Gilbert, Olive. *Narrative of Sojourner Truth.* Mineola, NY: Dover, 1997.

Green, Karen and Taormino, Tristan, eds. *A Girl's Guide to Taking Over the World.* New York: St. Martin's, 1997.

Golub, Sharon. *Periods: From Menarche to Menopause.* Newbury Park, CA: Sage Publications, 1992.

Graves, Robert. *The White Goddess.* New York: Farrar, Straus & Giroux, 1966.

Graves, Robert. *Mammon and the Black Goddess.* Garden City, NY: Doubleday, 1965.

Griffin, Susan. *A Chorus of Stones: The Private Life of War.* New York: Doubleday, 1992.

Guerrilla Girls. *Confessions of the Guerrilla Girls.* New York: Harper Perennial, 1995.

Harding, M. Esther. *Woman's Mysteries, Ancient and Modern.* New York: Harper & Row, 1976.

Haver, Ronald. *David O. Selznick's Hollywood.* New York: Knopf, 1980.

Hine, Darlene Clark, King, Wilma and Reed, Linda, eds. *We Specialize in the Wholly Impossible: A Reader in Black Women's History*. Brooklyn, NY: Carlson, 1995.

Hite, Shere. *Women as Revolutionary Agents of Change: The Hite Reports and Beyond*. Madison, WI: The University of Wisconsin Press, 1994.

Holiday, Billie (with William Dufty). *Lady Sings the Blues*. Garden City, NY: Doubleday, 1956.

hooks, bell. *Ain't I a Woman: Black Women and Feminism*. Boston, MA: SouthEnd Press, 1984.

hooks, bell. *A Woman's Mourning Song*. New York: Harlem River Press, 1993.

hooks, bell. *Wounds of Passion: A Writing Life*. New York: Holt, 1997.

Hulme, Keri. *The Bone People*. Baton Rouge: Louisiana State University Press, 1985.

Hurston, Zora Neale. *Their Eyes Were Watching God*. Urbana: University of Illinois Press, 1978.

Hurston, Zora Neale. *I Love Myself When I'm Laughing...And Then Again When I'm Looking Mean and Impressive*. Old Westbury, NY: The Feminist Press, 1979.

Jackson, LaToya. *Growing Up in the Jackson Family*. New York: Dutton, 1991.

Kaplan, Janet. *Unexpected Journeys: The Art and Life of Remedios Varo*. New York: Abbeville Press, 1988.

Khashoggi, Soheir. *Mirage*. New York: Forge, 1996.

Leamer, Laurence. *The Kennedy Women: The Saga of an American Family*. New York: Villiard, 1994.

Lerner, Gerda. *Black Women in White America: A Documentary History*. New York: Vintage, 1972.

Lindgren, Astrid. *Pippi Longstocking*. New York: Viking, 1950.

Lindgren, Astrid. *Pippi Goes On Board*. New York: Puffin, 1977.

Lindgren, Astrid. *Pippi Sails the South Seas*. New York: Viking, 1959.

Lord, M.G. *Forever Barbie; The Unauthorized Biography of a Real Doll*. New York: Avon, 1994.

Lorde, Audre. "Uses of the Erotic: The Erotic as Power" in Sister Outsider: Essays and Speeches. Trumansburg, NY: The Crossing Press, 1984.

Lorde, Audre. *I Am Your Sister: Black Women Organizing Across Sexualities*. New York: Kitchen Table, Women of Color Press, 1985.

Lunardini, Christine, Ph.D. *What Every American Should Know About Women's History*. Holbrook, MA: Bob Adams, Inc., 1994.

Lynn, Loretta (with George Vecsey). *Coal Miner's Daughter*. Chicago: Regnery, 1976.

Mankiller, Wilma (with Michael Wallis). *A Chief and Her People*. New York: St. Martin's, 1993.

Marx, Karl. *The Woman Question: Selections from the Writing of Fredrick Engels, V.I. Lenin, Joseph Stalin and Karl Marx*. New York: International Publishers, 1951.

Maus, Cynthia Pearl. *The World's Great Madonnas*. New York: Harper, 1947.

Mitchell, Margaret. *Gone With The Wind*. New York: MacMillan, 1939.

Morgan, Marlo. *Mutant Message Downunder.* Lees Summit, MO:
    MM Co., 1991.
Morrison, Toni. *Sula.* New York: Knopf, 1974.
Morrison, Toni. *Tar Baby.* New York: Knopf, 1981.
Morrison, Toni. *Beloved.* New York: Knopf, 1987.
Morrison, Toni. *The Bluest Eye.* New York: Knopf, 1993.

Nagel, Jill, ed. *Whores and Other Feminists.* New York: Routledge, 1997.

O'Connor, Flannery. *Wise Blood.* New York: Farrar, Straus &
    Cudahy, 1952.
O'Connor, Flannery. *Everything That Rises Must Converge.* New
    York: Farrar, Straus & Giroux, 1965.
Orenstein, Peggy. *SchoolGirls: Young Women, Self-Esteem, and the
    Confidence Gap.* New York: Doubleday, 1994.

Palmer, Rachel Lynn and Greensburg, Sarah K., M.D. *Facts and Frauds
    in Woman's Hygiene.* New York: The Vanguard Press, 1936.
Piercy, Marge. *Woman on the Edge of Time.* New York: Knopf, 1976.
Presley, Priscilla (with Sandra Harmon). *Elvis and Me.* New
    York: Putnam, 1985.

Queen, Carol. *Real Live Nude Girl.* San Francisco: Cleis, 1997.

Raymond, Janice G. *Women as Wombs: Reproductive Technologies
    and the Battle over Women's Freedom.* San Francisco:
    HarperSanFrancisco, 1993.
Redding, Judith M. and Brownworth, Victoria A. *Film Fatales:
    Independent Women Directors.* Seattle: Seal, 1997.

Roseanne. *Roseanne: My Life as a Woman*. City: Press, Year

Rothblatt, Martine. *The Apartheid of Sex: A Manifesto on the Freedom of Gender*. New York: Crown, 1995.

Sasson, Jean. *Princess Sultana*. New York: Morrow, 1992.

Sasson, Jean. *Princess Sultana's Daughters*. New York: Doubleday, 1994.

Scholz, Suzette, Stephanie and Sheri (with John Tullius). *Deep in the Heart of Texas: Reflections of Former Dallas Cowboy Cheerleaders*. New York: St. Martin's Press, 1991.

Sen, Mala. *The Bandit Queen*. New York: HarperCollins, 1995.

Sharp, Saundra. *Black Women for Beginners*. New York: Writers & Readers, 1993.

Silko, Leslie Marmon. *Almanac of the Dead and Ceremony*. New York: Simon & Schuster, 1991.

Silko, Leslie Marmon. *Ceremony*. New York: Penguin, 1986.

Smith, John M., M.D. *Women and Doctors: A Physicians Explosive Account of Women's Medical Treatment- and Mistreatment- in America Today and What You Can Do About It*. City: Press, Year

Solanas, Valerie. *S.C.U.M Manifesto*. London, U.K: Phoenix Press, 1991.

Tan, Amy. *The Joy Luck Club*. New York: Putnam, 1989.

Tan, Amy. *The Kitchen God's Wife*. New York: Putnam, 1991.

Taormino, Tristan. *The Ultimate Guide To Anal Sex for Women*. San Francisco: Cleis, 1997.

Tea, Michelle. *The Passionate Mistakes and Intimate Corruptions of One Girl in America*. New York: Semiotexte, 1998.

Walker, Alice. *The Color Purple*. New York: Harcourt, Brace, Jovanovich, 1982.

Walker, Alice and Parmar, Pratibha. *Warrior Marks: Female Genital Mutilation and the Sexual Blinding of Women.* New York: Harcourt, Brace, Jovanovich, 1993.

Walker, Barbara G. *The Women's Encyclopedia of Myths and Secrets.* San Francisco: Harper & Row, 1983.

Walker, Barbara G. *Crone: Woman of Age Wisdom and Power.* San Francisco: Harper & Row, 1985.

Winterson, Jeanette. *Art and Lies.* New York: Knopf, 1995.

Winterson, Jeanette. *Sexing the Cherry.* New York: Atlantic Monthly Press, 1990.

Winterson, Jeanette. *The Passion.* New York: Atlantic Monthly Press, 1988.

Woods, Beatrice. *I Shock Myself.* San Francisco: Chronicle Books, 1988.

Woods, Donald. *Biko.* New York: Vintage, 1979.

Woodson, Jacqueline. *Autobiography of a Family Photo: A Novel.* New York: Dutton, 1995.

Woodson, Jacqueline. *I Hadn't Meant to Tell You This.* New York: Delacorte, 1994.

X, Malcolm and Haley, Alex. *The Autobiography of Malcolm X.* New York: Grove, 1965.

Yoshimoto, Banana. *Kitchen.* New York: Grove, 1993.

Zahavi, Helen. *The Weekend.* New York: Donald I. Fine, 1991.

Zinn, Howard. *A People's History of the United States, 1492-Present.* New York: HarperPerennial, 1995.

Credits

Gracious Thanks

Writers tend to put acknowledgment pages in their books because—unless authored by the very vain or very hermetic—books do not come to fruition without the support and love of many, many individuals.

In college, I learned the value of unqualified support from a single human being. Dr. Leo Daugherty read my stories, poems, essays and interviews with a sensitivity and insight I hadn't experienced since elementary school, when Mrs. Lingle and Mrs. House—my second and third grade teachers, respectively—prodded my imagination with a gusto I was wholly unappreciative of at the time. I extend my deepest regards to these three educators.

From the outset of this book, Holly Marie Morris was the single human being who believed in me so much my heart *positively swells*. Trust and respect are huge gifts. I do not take lightly Holly's inspiration for bringing these gifts into my life. *Cunt* would never, ever, ever have been written if I hadn't seen her that day in New York, gliding 'cross the room in her cream linen suit like grace was a word made 'specially with her in mind. Holly, I love you dearly.

My mother was the first person to read an early draft of *Cunt*. Because her experiences are so integral to my writing, I hoped to procure her blessing before venturing on to a rewrite. Not only is my mother from a different culture, but many of my beliefs are difficult for someone of her generation to understand. Regardless, she never paused in support of my words. She did not ask me to edit out a single iota of her life experiences. Her courage overwhelms me. I am honored to be her daughter.

I gave the final draft of *Cunt* to my brother, Joe B., and my sister, Elizabeth, for Christmas 1997. A man of few words, my brother left a concise message on my voice mail two weeks later, "It's killer," he said. "Goddamn, this is just killer." My sister, a person I have aptly nicknamed "Hard Customer," called me at least twice a week for a month, gushing with excitement and love.

Obviously, Joe B. and Liz are my siblings and lot of people might think, *"Of course* they had nice things to say," but it is an absolute veracity that my brother and sister would never say things to spare my feelings. If there's shit to be talked, rest assured, they are the first to talk it.

I don't thank them solely for reading my book with such care and devotion, I thank them for letting me know I am as precious to them as they are to me. It is extremely painful that we learned the preciousness of life through the death of our brother, but all the same, I am glad we learned this.

Jennie Goode and Faith Conlon. Goode and Faith, need I say more? Their Goode Faith in *Cunt* deserves accolades of candy and champagne forever. I know it is considered a "risk" to publish this book, and they, along with the entire staff of Seal Press—Lee Damsky, Ingrid Emerick, Laura Gronewold, Kate Loeb, Lisa Okey and Lynn Siniscalchi—rose to the occasion like prima ballerinas aloft. And don't even get me started on Jennie Goode's paranormal levels of comprehension. Lordisa.

Likewise, many thanks to Leigh Feldman. Her belief in this project was—given the aforementioned "risk" factor—astounding.

I will never forget the day she told me she felt like standing on the rooftop screaming "cunt" at the top of her lungs. Thank you. You rule.

Loraine Harkin, naturopathic physician, kindly read the manuscript and shared her knowledge. Her input and support for *Cunt* were greatly appreciated.

When it was time to get jacket and press photos taken, I went with a gut feeling and called Rebecca McBride. The resulting photographs freaked me out. It was as if she prowled around in my dreamworld and somehow duplicated the precise images I could conjure only nebulous words to describe. Rebecca is a genius.

Sybil, Paul, Memphis, Erin and Christopher were so kind to me during a very difficult time. Ditto Peri Heydari Pakroo, Oh My!, Turtle, Parisha and Jason Speewhoreski.

Lisa Vogel and the Michigan Womyn's Music Festival inspired me and goaded me on in ways I'm sure they are completely unaware of.

Whenever I feel like maybe there's no magic in the world, maybe I've been wrong this whole time, I just think of Panacea and Mr. Quintron, and I know there are always spells to cast and pussycats to cavort with.

Om. Her voice, her love, her letters from Japan. How I love Om. Elizabeth Faye spoils her women with laughter and massages. Gasperini sends her women skateboards in the mail, which makes them have total spontaneous orgasms of joy. Dawn Kiss, the beautiful, passionate snowboarding punk rock valkyrie ablaze.

Bridget Irish, 100 percent Irish, born on St. Patrick's Day. Bridget tells me I can do anything I want. When voices in my head say stuff like, "Inga, you *can't* call him 'Keith "Piece of Shit" Richards,'" Bridget's face floats into my frontal lobe, and I *know,* I can call him "Keith 'Piece of Feral Dogshit Smeared on the Washington Monument' Richards," if I want.

I am intensely grateful for the support and love of dearest Kotexi, Bart, Mrs. L. and Dr. Flusty.

If home is where the heart is, my heart is where Bambi, Shug, Sini and Alisun are. All four of my housemates listened to me wrestle with various chapters, put up with my freakish hours and respected the importance of bunny ears. My week *sucks* if Bambi and I don't have our Sunday morning coffee 'n smokes session. Shug's bright, blazing smile is a pillar of our community. I could listen to Sini's hilarious stories for hours on end. Alisun's logical mind has improved the quality of my life hundreds of times. She never misses a *follicle* of inconsistency.

I love you all so very much.

And the genius filmmaker, Harperetta Carter. My heart *grieves* for those who underestimate her scathing perspective on life and society, which she cleverly hides in her sweet, sweet smile and grandmother-spiced tenderness.

At three o' clock in the morning, when I *hafta* share something, to cry or hear a beautiful story, I call Riz, my sunshine in the dead of night. He never gets mad at me even if I wake him up. He is groggy for a few minutes and then swings right into a tirade about love, Oprah, his Grandmother. If I was stuck on my book, I always knew somehow or other Riz would unstick me.

The psycho-enchanting and beautiful Ali Ø. brought into my life—among many exemplary things—the following sentence: "You don't get what you deserve, you get what you negotiate." For that little gem alone, I am forever indebted to her.

Kinnie Starr, Toni Childs, Diamanda Galás, Me'Shell NdegéOcello, Sinéad O'Connor, Tracy Chapman, the Immortal Caruso and Chet Baker: I wore out their CDs working on my book. I wore out the repeat button on my CD player. I disgusted neighbors who wondered what kind of freckin' fruitcake would listen to the same goddamn CD for six hours straight, night after night. I thank them for making music in the world. Diamanda, especially, helped me with the chapter on rape. It was the most painful one for me to write and without Diamanda's presence in my kitchen, I don't know how I could have managed.

Also, Fiona Apple. In her song "Never is a Promise" she sings, "My fever burns me deeper than I've ever shown." I thank her for putting a simple sentence behind a complex feeling that drives this book.

gracious thanks

About the Author

Inga Muscio is a reclusive, self-styled literary magnate who writes books so she doesn't lose touch with the lower echelons of society. On her father's side, Ms. Muscio is a fourth-generation Swiss-Italian, born in Santa Maria, California. Her mother is an Irish immigrant and always pronounces words wrong. If you are ever fortunate enough to see Ms. Muscio conduct a book reading, you will probably notice she inherited this affliction.

Ms. Muscio's writing has appeared in *Bust, Curve* and numerous other publications. She has contributed to anthologies and is the music editor for *W.I.G.* magazine. She presently lives in San Francisco, where she shamelessly displays her overbite to beautiful women and rides around town on either her bike ("Bikey") or her skateboard ("Boardie"). As is evidenced by the title of her first book, Inga Muscio's vernacular is comparable to that of a merchant marine.

Selected Titles from Seal Press

Adiós, Barbie: Young Women Write About Body Image and Identity edited by Ophira Edut. $14.95, 1-58005-016-6. Essays filled with honesty and humor by women who have chosen to ignore, subvert or redefine the dominant beauty standard.

Listen Up: Voices from the Next Feminist Generation edited by Barbara Findlen. $14.95, 1-878067-61-3. The voices of today's young feminists are brought together to explore and reveal their lives.

Film Fatales: Independent Women Directors by Judith M. Redding and Victoria A. Brownworth. $16.95, 1-878067-97-4. Includes profiles of over thirty pioneering directors, producers and distributors who have changed the face of contemporary film.

SurferGrrrls: Look, Ethel! An Internet Guide for Us! by Laurel Gilbert and Crystal Kile, with illustrations by Ellen Forney. $15.00, 1-878067-79-6. Provides fabulous online resources for women and girls and a vast cyberculture repertoire.

Wired Women: Gender and New Realities in Cyberspace edited by Lynn Cherny and Elizabeth Reba Weise. $16.00, 1-878067-73-7. A provocative and impassioned look at what women are doing on the net.

She's A Rebel: The History of Women in Rock & Roll by Gillian G. Gaar. $16.95, 1-878067-08-7. *She's A Rebel* tells the fascinating story of the women who have shaped rock and pop music for the last five decades.

Lap Dancing for Mommy: Tender Stories of Disgust, Blame and Inspiration by Erika Lopez. 1-878067-96-6, $14.00. These incisive comic narratives offer reams of racy, raunchy and riotous appeal.

ess publishes many books of fiction and nonfiction by
s. To receive a free catalog or order from us
call our toll-free orders number at 800-754-0271.
 at www.sealpress.com.